Praise for The *[Art of Spiritual Writing]*

"Here, gathered in one careful, one clear, personable, experie anybody ever needs to know abo_____ ____ *field of religion and spirituality. I cannot praise it too highly."*

—Phyllis Tickle, author of *Emergence Christianity*

"*By far the best book I've ever read on the difficulties and special joys of the spiritual writing vocation.*"

—Paula Huston, author of *The Holy Way, Simplifying the Soul,* and *A Season of Mystery*

"The Art of Spiritual Writing *shows why her peers regard Vinita Hampton Wright as one of the best editors and writers of spiritual books working today. It is a guide to wisdom as well as craft, and sure to become a standard in the field.*"

—Michael Leach, publisher emeritus of Orbis Books

"*A veritable treasure trove of wise and practical guidance for anyone who, in Vinita's words, feels called to turn their own story into a story for others. Essential and enjoyable reading for every aspiring writer.*"

—Margaret Silf, author of *Inner Compass* and *The Other Side of Chaos*

"*If you aspire to use the written word to share your heart with others, do yourself a favor and read this book.*"

—Tim Muldoon, author of *The Ignatian Workout* and *Longing to Love*

Other Books by Vinita Hampton Wright

Nonfiction

The Soul Tells a Story: Engaging Creativity with Spirituality in the Writing Life

Days of Deepening Friendship: For the Woman Who Wants Authentic Life with God

Simple Acts of Moving Forward: 60 Suggestions for Getting Unstuck

Praying Freedom: A Book of Lenten Meditations

The St. Thérèse of Lisieux Prayer Book

Fiction

Grace at Bender Springs

Velma Still Cooks in Leeway

Dwelling Places

Allen AUG 18

The Art of Spiritual Writing

How to Craft Prose That Engages and Inspires Your Readers

VINITA HAMPTON WRIGHT

LOYOLA PRESS.
A JESUIT MINISTRY

Chicago

LOYOLA PRESS.
A JESUIT MINISTRY

3441 N. Ashland Avenue
Chicago, Illinois 60657
(800) 621-1008
www.loyolapress.com

Cover art credit: Simon Oxley/iStockPhoto.com/ThinkStock

ISBN-13: 978-0-8294-3908-3
ISBN-10: 0-8294-3908-0
Library of Congress Control Number: 2013943382

Printed in the United States of America.

13 14 15 16 17 18 Bang 10 9 8 7 6 5 4 3 2 1

Contents

First of All

First of all, you need to know that this book is a manual. For more than two decades I have advised writers and edited their work for the spirituality market. Now I have tried to distill the best of what I know for those writers who hope to serve people's spiritual needs. You won't find stunning prose here—mainly I provide lists and short paragraphs designed to instruct and help.

If you have spent many years reading books, you probably remember the day a mere paragraph changed your life. Perhaps you have experienced multiple conversions while at the mercy of words on a page. Good writing can do that. Spiritually astute writing has that kind of power.

You have picked up this particular book, an indication that you desire to write life-changing prose and, perhaps, publish it. You want to inspire, inform, challenge, or delight the person who takes in your phrases and stories. You hope to write paragraphs that set fire to readers' souls, the kind of paragraphs that people underline and take to heart.

Such writing is deceptive because it takes hard work, but once that work is done, the sentences and phrases read as if they came naturally and without effort. That's why we call writing a craft—you have to become good at it. If you don't become skilled at the craft, you simply won't reach the heart and mind of your reader. Instead, you will bore the reader and muddy the idea and get in the way of the writer-to-reader encounter that leads to inspiration and transformation.

Several years ago, I wrote another book, *The Soul Tells a Story: Engaging Creativity with Spirituality in the Writing Life*. That book explores the creative process in more depth, was written to inspire and encourage, and in places has a measured, contemplative feel. If you want to understand your creative process better and learn how to do the whole-life work of a writer, I suggest you first go to *The Soul Tells a Story*. I tell more stories in that book. Actually, I use a sweeter voice in that one, too.

If you're ready to get to the business of writing and publishing, however, keep reading.

A significant number of the suggestions in *The Art of Spiritual Writing* are given to help you make your writing more marketable. As an editor for a Jesuit publisher for the past decade, I have seen a good deal of writing cross my desk. My editor colleagues and I feel that many writers have important things to say but are not knowledgeable about what it takes to write for an audience beyond family and friends. These are the issues we deal with daily as manuscripts and proposals come to us. That lack of knowledge in potential authors is the primary reason we turn down manuscripts.

In *The Art of Spiritual Writing*, I try to help you get the job done. I presume that you are already inspired and have something to say; the goal is to help you say it effectively and get it published.

So, let's get to it.

1

What Does It Mean to "Write" Spirituality?

Let's not worry too much over definitions, because spirituality is as diverse as the people who try to practice it, and writing manifests in almost as many styles. It is important, however, to identify the qualities that mark both fiction and nonfiction writing as spiritual—as relevant to interior, intentional development. How shall we describe spiritual writing?

Spiritual writing is true.

It compels us to see the truth and worry over the truth and allow the truth to change us. Sometimes we must reassess what we have seen as truth and believed to be the truth. Sometimes we must see truth from another's viewpoint, which will

1

reframe truth that for years was familiar and comfortable and that required little from us.

Spiritual writing is courageous.

Otherwise it could never deal with the truth. Were spiritual writing not courageous, it would be impossible to do the hard work that makes the writing worthy of the label "spiritual." Courage goes straight to the question and unease; courage allows confrontation and disassembling so that the new thing can be created. Courage also does not care much about prevailing opinions but writes what must be written.

Spiritual writing is hopeful.

A writer of spiritual work believes that life is worth writing about. He or she believes that reflection and exploration will reap benefits. The spiritual writer communicates for the sake of uplifting the world, celebrating it, opening its depths, revealing its wonders, and healing its wounds.

Spiritual writing is engaging.

Because my day job for more than a decade has been editing books for a Jesuit publisher, I have become well acquainted with the principles of Ignatian spirituality. The Jesuit order of Catholic priests—also known as the Society of Jesus—was founded way back in 1539 by St. Ignatius of Loyola and several companions. Ignatius's most well-known writing, *The Spiritual Exercises*, became foundational to what many of us know as spiritual direction. I could go on at length about Ignatius's insights, but I mention him in this book because he understood that the spiritual life is an ongoing engagement with reality. He understood that prayer must always be an experience, not merely an idea or a belief.

As a writer and one who has assisted many other writers, I have learned that creativity also is bold engagement. Good "spirituality" writing creates an experience for the reader and makes demands on the reader, but only after it has done all of that to the writer. True creativity is a spiritual function, a form of engagement that requires openness, attentiveness, honesty, and desire. These same traits are necessary for spiritual growth and enlightenment. The best spiritual writing is what I would call thoroughly Ignatian in that it creates an experience for the reader. This sort of writing goes further than providing information or giving instructions; it creates a space of engagement in which the reader might connect to reality and be moved forward into her life and gifts.

So when you bring together the act of writing with the realm of spirituality, you have encountered *engagement* in one of its finest embodiments. "Spirituality writing" transcends words on the page, yet it forms through words. When a writer takes on the task of exploring the world of the spirit, she has invited a process that will change her permanently. If she has done her work well, it will change her readers, too.

- How do we bring together our most interior sensitivities with the concrete experiences we create by arranging words into sentences, pages, and entire visions?
- How do we tame the fiery truths of the universe by giving them names or descriptions? Should we even try?

I believe that, for some of us, attempting to juggle fire is a life calling. A writer's task is to discover the names of things, and the task of a spirituality writer is to provide vocabulary by which the rest of us can name what God—that lovely, terrifying Divine—is doing to us, for us, around us, and right inside us.

What follows are a few chapters to help the writer who feels compelled to invite this quite spiritual process in which she lays out, in phrases and paragraphs, the realm where human meets Divine, where we truly engage and then tell the story of what happened.

2

The First Five Things Every Spirituality Writer Needs to Know

Writers of spirituality are already at a disadvantage because they have passion and, to a certain extent, missionary zeal, even if the goal isn't any form of saving souls. The message is important, and the drive to help or enlighten readers can give the writer tunnel vision. Too easily can the focus become an agenda; when that happens, the importance of the content might announce itself too loudly, overwhelming nuance and craft.

So the writer of "spirituality" has no choice but to be brutal in assessing the work. Having read many proposals and edited scores of manuscripts written on spirituality, I can with confidence offer five statements that are nearly always true when it comes to composing a work that will connect with the reader.

Nothing makes up for poor craftsmanship.

Writing is a craft, and it is a different form of expression from speaking, teaching, or preaching. Those forms have their own purposes, and they also have rules of engagement that work for them specifically. When you deliver words in person through speaking, the audience can rely on your facial expressions, tones and inflections of voice, and gestures to help them understand what you're saying with your words. If you say something incorrectly or in half-sentences and phrases oddly hung together—all fairly normal occurrences in spoken communication—your listeners will likely understand what you mean because of the other cues.

When you write, however, the only indicators of meaning are the words on the page and how they are arranged and punctuated. Once all of these are printed, there's no going back; even digital files that are used on various electronic readers must go through a correction process, leaving errors to linger and confuse readers in the meantime.

In written communication, everything that appears on the page matters; each word and punctuation mark must have a purpose. Also, everything on that page has the potential to change the meaning or obscure the meaning. This means that anything written must follow the rules that make written words understandable: grammar, spelling, punctuation, sentence structure, and the words themselves.

So, learn to write, and write well. Don't assume that because you give a breathtaking lecture you are already competent to write those same ideas with equal force and clarity. Improving your writing craft will take work, but it doesn't require genius; there are hundreds of books on grammar and basic writing skills. Some of them offer useful writing exercises that help you apply the concepts and practice them. If you can afford it and feel the need, attend courses on writing—these, too, are everywhere, especially online. You don't have to spend a fortune unless you really want to go to some exotic location for an extended workshop with a famous instructor. The nuts and bolts of writing are available for the price of a few good instructional manuals. And the nuts and bolts will take you a long way. If you do go to an expensive and inspiring workshop on writing, you'll get a lot more out of it if you have done your nuts-and-bolts work beforehand. Having mastered the basic skills and rules, you then will be freer to follow the ideas inspired by speakers and scenic locales.

If you sign a contract with a publisher, don't plan to lean heavily on editors and proofreaders to clean up your writing clutter. If you're very lucky, you'll have an editor who has the luxury to go through your work line by line and with great care. But often the publishing industry cuts corners on editing time. Your material needs to be really good before an editor ever gets her hands on it. Remember this, too: the more editing your work needs, the more likely the editor will introduce errors because what you wrote has left too much open to interpretation. A heavy edit nearly always means another run-through by both author and editor, making changes to the changes. This turns into a compromised schedule and too much rushing around close to publication time. Better to save yourself and your publisher the stress and irritation.

You may have a great story or message, but if it is badly crafted, the story gets lost and the reader loses interest.

Save teaching for the classroom and preaching for the pulpit.

If a person wants to be taught, he will take a class. When that same person picks up a book, he expects a different experience. An article or book should not sound like a person standing at the front of the room passing out information. Of course, you *are* providing information, but the way you do it is crucial. You want to write so that the matter unfolds and the reader experiences the unfolding. You explore a topic, and the reader comes right along with you.

You may be an authority on the topic, but don't rely on your authority to hold anyone's interest. The writing itself must be seductive. Even a good self-help book avoids sounding forceful and instead makes the reader feel respected and invited. For instance, I'm writing this book you are reading in a get-to-the-point, instructional way; nevertheless, if you are already skimming and looking ahead to other headings and chapters, I've done a bad job here. Even as I give straightforward information, I need constantly to pull you in. I may advise you quite bluntly, because this is a writing manual, not a devotional book. But if I come across as too know-it-all, you'll drop this book and not pick it up again.

People who enjoy being preached at generally are not looking for books that will engage and challenge them; they seek books that reinforce what they already believe. They seek books that make them feel right and safe. Books that encourage them to ask questions make them uneasy. Books that help them open the spiritual doors to mystery and anything new become suspect. If you desire to write effectively on spiritual themes, this is not the audience you seek. And so if you write in a preachy, didactic, and overbearing way, you will attract the audience you don't want, and you'll repel the audience you hope for.

When someone feels preached at while reading a book, unless she is desperate for the information or already believes she deserves to be preached at and belittled, she will simply stop reading.

This doesn't mean that you can't write with authority. Lay out your ideas clearly, without waffling or qualifications. In fact, when you get rid of excessive prose, which often is present in poor writing, your words automatically will ring more true.

Keep in mind that authoritative writing does not consist exclusively of making statements and constructing good arguments. The authority issues from the writer's competence and attitude. You can form questions and posit ideas, all quite inviting to the reader, and the reader will track with you and trust you. You can also write about your personal struggles and doubts and questions without losing the respect or attention of the reader.

Fiction is about storytelling, not teaching.

Some of our most spiritual literature exists in the form of novels and short stories. Any good novel or short story teaches us something, but the way we learn from fiction is different from the way we learn a subject or a skill. What we gain from a story affects a different part of the brain entirely. Any work of fiction that is structured to teach will fail as fiction—that is, as a work of art. Any work of fiction that is driven by a message or an agenda will fail as good storytelling. Fiction is not meant to teach, drive an agenda, or deliver a message.

For example, in nonfiction writing, often we are building an argument or a system of thinking. The structure is probably linear, with one point leading naturally to the next. In fiction, the momentum grows out of conflict and mystery. The protagonist has a desire and strives to fulfill it, but things keep getting in the way. And if the protagonist is presented in a realistic way, then he doesn't get all the information he needs, and he certainly doesn't get it in the right order—because real life seldom works that way. But it's the reader's emotional attachment to the possible good outcome that keeps her engaged. We seem to be designed to love problem solving and mystery unraveling in the story of a protagonist. In fact, it's the withheld information that keeps us reading—and happily so. However, a nonfiction book created in the same way—winding around obstacles and missing puzzle pieces—will more likely frustrate the reader, who wishes we would get to the point, please.

Powerful fiction develops out of characters and situations that are authentic. Fiction is also an art form unto itself. To paraphrase John Gardner, author of the classic *The Art of Fiction*: when you write fiction, you create a dream, and the goal is to write in such a way that the reader doesn't wake up until the very end of the dream, the very last page of the book. Excellent craftsmanship is essential for this kind of seamless and riveting writing. I have written fiction and nonfiction, and although the craft of writing is the same for both—the sentences have to work, the words must be chosen with care—the process for the two types of writing is not entirely the same.

If you are a spirituality writer who is venturing into fiction, then it's important that you learn from excellent fiction writers. Read high-quality novels and short stories. Go to the best writers and teachers, regardless of what you may think of their worldview or their brand of spirituality. One of my best writing teachers quite clearly did not share my beliefs. But he knew how to teach craftsmanship. Also, he liked me—a fairly vocal Christian—because I respected the craft of writing and did not allow my beliefs or worldview to disrupt the simple hard work of handling words on a page.

The reader becomes engaged when she has to do some of the work.

Effective spirituality writing invites the reader to engage. This means that everything isn't spelled out. It means that sometimes, rather than offer answers, you open up the questions. Those of us who write from a Christian worldview must remember that we actually believe the Holy Spirit is already on the job, and that drawing people to truth, or enlightenment, or resolution, is not all up to us.

If you want readers to be drawn to your work and to appreciate what you have to offer, then invite them to participate in a process of discovery. This is an open-ended process over which you have little control—and that's the way it *should* be. Here are a few suggestions for encouraging reader engagement.

- Use anecdotes and illustrations to which the reader can relate and that will elicit emotional responses.

- With care and sensitivity, name the issue or the experience. Your job as a writer is to articulate and give vocabulary to human experience. When you do this, the reader will recognize that experience as her own, or as what might become her own, and she will stay with you as you continue to articulate and name the experience.

- Make the writing sensual—write in a way that stimulates sight, touch, taste, hearing, and smell. Readers are physical—they are ensouled bodies—and the best writing relates to them as such.

- Pose questions rather than answers.

- Make suggestions, not declarations.

- Be honest—don't be afraid to let your own humanity show. People aren't interested in reading about someone who appears to be better than they are—who is smarter, more together, more successful, or more adventurous. Write so that the reader can imagine herself in your situation and growing right along with you.

- Write with some balance. That is, be honest but hopeful. Be encouraging but challenging.

It's really important not to wrap up a topic as if everything is solved and understood. In real life, this is never the case. Especially in spiritual development, the understanding is ongoing; it takes a lot of turns, and sometimes it backtracks. You're not giving the reader a definitive map of a spiritual process; you are providing some company along the way.

Personal writing must be transformed in order to work as public writing.

When we read an article or memoir that is truly interesting and illuminating, it's impossible for us to see all the work that made the writing so effective. It might read as if it's right out of a journal or simply told from memory. But—trust me on this—personal writing that reaches other people has gone through a strenuous process of editing and rewriting. There are undoubtedly a few exceptions, but it's probably best if you and I presume that we are not the exceptions.

When it comes to your own story, many of the details that are important to you will be meaningless to readers. For you, the chronology may be important, but to the readers, theme is primary. All the thinking and feeling that led up to a certain decision or conversation is part of the history you know, but the reader may not need to know about all the thinking and feeling you experienced. Nothing can feel quite so wearying as reading through the description of interior details of someone's life—the unending tumble of memories, emotions, questions, and inner dialogues. After a page or two, the reader is seriously beginning not to care. Your task is to pick and choose among the thousands of details, standing back from the story to understand what a stranger would need to know and what would capture the stranger's interest.

Also, as a writer you must come to a point of distance from what you are writing about. The reader can't be burdened with whatever emotional baggage you're carrying. Writing that is angry, bitter, self-centered, or whiney just will not be appealing or acceptable to most readers. This doesn't mean that you drop the emotional material from the writing or that you brush past the emotions. Good writing is emotionally honest but does not get stuck in the emotion.

Accept that you will never be objective enough to judge your personal writing very well. During the writing process you will need review readers who are honest and who know something about good writing. You'll need to listen to them and do the work of revision.

3

Understanding the Difference between Personal and Public Writing

I've lost track of all the manuscripts that have come to my editorial desk from people who survived tragedy, who processed the experience through writing, and who then came to feel strongly that their written accounts would help others dealing with a similar tragedy. We editors dread the arrival of such manuscripts because we know that (1) 98 percent of these are not publishable and (2) regardless of their quality, they needed to be written. *That is, people often need to process their lives by writing about their experiences, but needing to write is not the same as writing something that should be published.*

That sounds cold, but honesty will take people further than polite denial will, and my desire is for people to move forward, whatever their situation. So, for anyone out there who wants to understand the difference between personal and public writing, here's what I've tried to communicate through more than a few carefully written rejection letters.

Personal writing is for the person doing the writing.

When you are working through your life situation, the writing you do is first of all for you and no one else. A lot of people process life through journal writing, but other kinds of writing can help just as much. I've written stories that were not publishable but that did my own soul some good. All professional writers have material that remains unpublished—stories, articles, sometimes entire novels. A lot of poetry falls into this category—Lord knows, I've written enough of it. I have a couple of friends who enjoy reading my amateur poetry, and that's audience enough. If I were to try to publish my poetry, this endeavor would involve a whole new process of learning to write according to the rules of good poetry, learning how to evaluate my work, and rewriting and perfecting. My most powerful poems have helped me name something I needed to identify for my own growth. In terms of literary quality, they were not so powerful, and certainly they were not written well enough for publication.

Personal writing is too specific to one situation to translate well to anyone else's situation.

When you arrive at the juncture of trying to sell a proposal or manuscript, one of the first two or three questions the potential publisher will ask is, Who's your audience?

If you can't identify the audience, then you will have great difficulty getting anyone to partner with you on publication. The people to whom and for whom you are writing will help you shape the work. The audience will determine how the chapters are organized, which promises you make to the reader, what the best title will be, and how the book will be marketed. All these factors are weighed and debated in publication meetings. Out of the millions of potential readers out in the world, which group will merit a sales and marketing budget?

For instance, all the details of Molly's battle with cancer are Molly's details alone. Although many other cancer patients will share some of that experience, they don't necessarily benefit from reading about Molly's journey exactly as she recalls it. Support groups provide the stories, companionship, and suggestions that people who are suffering a similar illness need. Usually a written story won't work as well. And often, what you really have is a magazine article that could be much more helpful than a full-fledged book. Even then, it must be shaped into an article to which many people can relate.

This principle of specific versus general is quite tricky, because if I communicate the right specifics of my situation, then the reader will relate to me better than if I had been more general and all-encompassing. For instance, miscarriage is a common tragedy. Every situation will have its unique points. One woman miscarries after a long series of infertility treatments; another miscarries a child between two other normal births. As a woman who has experienced miscarriage myself, I may not relate to the circumstances of the miscarriages; what will touch me at that deep, painful wound will be each woman's description of trying to grieve. What if the pregnancy is so short that there is no funeral? What if other family members try to pass it off as not such a big deal? The specifics of grieving will be key more than the stories about lengthy medical procedures or about the detailed live births of other children.

Now, if you're writing a book on infertility, that focus will determine which specifics are important to draw in the readers who have picked up a book on infertility. In this case, what the readers need and want are the very details about procedures that the readers of the miscarriage book don't care about so much. Do you see what I'm getting at here? The audience and the focus of the book must determine which personal specifics are appropriate for inclusion.

Personal writing, however, will include the details *you* need, and you owe it to your own spiritual health to write what you need and not worry about potential readers. It's important that you do the writing you need; focus on that first of all.

Personal writing helps those close to the event make some sense of it.

Most of the time, readers outside the event's circle don't have the same need to make sense of that specific event. The audience for most tragedies is a limited one; even if a million other women watch their children die of a certain disease, not all of them will want to read about someone else's experience with that. Each of them is already grappling with her distinct search for meaning in the context of tragedy. Within a family, faith community, or circle of friends, tragedy and trauma are worked out through much storytelling. Various people tell the story of how they have experienced the tragedy, and most people feel the need to tell the story numerous times. The storytelling is part of the healing, and it works quite effectively.

However, storytelling is not the same as writing a book about what has happened. Usually the storytelling helps people process and heal. After time has passed and healing has progressed, the need for storytelling is not as intense; of course, we continue to tell our stories for years to come, but the need to repeat them is not so strong or frequent. But if, during that early stage of grieving, the people involved try to write a book for publication, their strong emotions and their need for telling the story will likely fog the writing process. While they are trying to write for others, they really should be storytelling for themselves. In such cases, trying to write for publication and deal with the demands of editing and marketing can become more frustrating than healing.

At the very least, personal stories need time before they can become public stories. My editor alarms go off when I'm approached by someone who has recently come through a situation she deems worthy of writing about. Whether she's recently widowed, divorced, cured of cancer, or has lost a child, the chances are slim that she has healed and processed enough personally to work with the raw material of her battered life for the purpose of unseen and disinterested potential readers. Sometimes a professional writer who specializes in memoir can handle such a task, but most people who try to write this kind of book are not seasoned writers and have not been trained in the genre of memoir.

Personal writing has a specific purpose and needs no other justification.

In grieving for my deceased father, I wrote some eloquent words. But those writings moved in a direction I needed them to move, and I don't expect many other people to have exactly that same need. We need to allow ourselves plenty of time and space to journal and write poetry and essays and songs and whatever else we need to generate for the process we're experiencing. No one needs an excuse to do that kind of writing. Writing that helps us work through life events needs no other justification. So, write. Write as much as you need to. Allow the writing to do the work it's meant to do. Don't burden this writing with an added agenda of publication, fame, or outside validation.

Personal writing is usually emotional, passionate, and tunnel-visioned.

This is as it should be, because the writer is working through emotions, living out of her deepest passions, and she doesn't need to see anything but what she must focus on. However, when it comes to public writing, readers need more even-tempered material. They need content with focus broad enough to include their own experiences.

How is public writing different from what I've just described as personal writing?

Public writing requires time to gestate and develop from the initial writing that generated it.

Years ago I lost my only pregnancy to miscarriage. I was journaling about it all along, and I wrote several versions of an article that I thought would help other women who experienced miscarriage. As an editor, though, I knew that this article was not ready for the public. It needed more time. *I* needed more time. It took me five years to produce a publishable version of this material. It takes time to gain enough objectivity from your own experience to shape the material for the benefit of others. There are a few gifted writers who seem to have a miraculously short process time for effective personal-to-public writing. I'm certainly not one of them. Most writers do not fall into that category.

Public writing is shaped for the readers, not for the person writing it.

This means that many of the details and nuances meaningful to the writer get edited out. The structure gets reworked. I have to imagine what would motivate a person to read this piece—and I have to imagine what that person would expect to get out of it. Once I answer those two questions, my task as a writer is to shape the work accordingly—which often means that I am ruthless toward my own needs and preferences. Whole paragraphs will disappear. The tone will change as well, to be welcoming and respectful to the readers rather than merely expressive of my own passions.

Public writing takes the concrete details of a single, personal experience to generate a discussion of the more universal experience readers will relate to.

This aspect of writing takes a lot of nuance, because the writer is using personal details but they are carefully selected ones. The end result is that they don't point so much toward the writer's experience as they evoke in the readers' minds their own experiences that fall into the same category. *To write more universally is not to write in more general terms.* Here is where, in the world of essays, the truly skilled writers shine above the rest of us. They manage to choose just the right details. They unfold very personal experience in such a way that the reader feels as if her own life is being described.

It's so difficult to understand which details are the right details that I believe you come to the right details only by rewriting and rewriting and rewriting. Numerous revisions will help you sort out the best words and anecdotes.

To conclude, I must say this: Please write what and when you need to write. Write for yourself. Write for those people close to you. Write until you accomplish within yourself what needs to happen.

Then put it away for a while—maybe even a year or two. Take it out and read it and look for clues that the world out there might benefit from this story or reflection. Then do the work that must be done. I wish you well, because, in my opinion, this is the hardest writing of all. When we manage to do it well, the result is powerful and beautifully rich.

4

How to Make Your Story a Story for Others

Around my workplace, we often refer to our mission as "people for others." St. Ignatius and his companions formed the Society of Jesus for the purpose of "helping souls." Helping souls is at the heart of what most spirituality publishers are about. By definition, writing that is aimed at people who are either "spiritual" or "religious" endeavors to help them in their spiritual development.

Writing is quite a solitary experience. The words begin in one person's mind and out of that person's interest or passion. Then, when it's in the process of publication, this spirituality writing becomes a business venture, because even not-for-profit publishing houses must stay in business.

So even though it's a big deal to write a story, it's an even bigger deal to make it a story for others. In pulling that off, the writer must transcend her individual realm and deliver something that the publisher can market and sell. What a world.

My job is helping writers turn *their* stories into stories for others. Here are a few things I've learned along the way.

Understand that what helps you write the story will not necessarily help someone else read the story.

This is a real shift in the writer's thinking, but it can make a huge difference in the final result.

The introduction or first chapter you write in order to get into the topic—in order to get yourself going—often will not be the introduction a reader needs to get going. This means that you'll likely dump the introductory material or severely rewrite it.

The chapter titles that help you shape the work may not be the chapter titles that capture the attention of potential readers. Consider chapter titles primarily to be marketing tools. If the potential reader is not captivated by the mere Table of Contents, then you've already lost the sale. Especially now that increasingly more sales are in the digital market—where the cover is not as visible and immediate, and where the book description on the back cover has no place to hang its hat, as the back cover is nonexistent—the Table of Contents has to sell the book. Thus, the chapter titles must be composed with the reader in mind.

The Scriptures, quotes from other sources, and various other devices that inspire you or otherwise help you put the manuscript together may not be necessary in the final version that others will read. I structured my entire third novel on the stanzas of an old hymn. All the time I was writing the novel, those five stanzas stood at the beginning of the five parts of the book. I even had a CD of the hymn playing much of the time I was writing. These stanzas remained all the way through the rewrites and the edit. It was toward the end of the edit when I told my editor to dump those stanzas because they would not be as meaningful to the readers as they were to me, and they would clutter the pages. The editor agreed with me. It could just have easily have been the editor who noticed this. Listen to the editor and other readers when they say that you can trim out such material.

The vision or metaphor or life-changing experience that sets you on the path to write the story may have little meaning to readers; it will likely need to remain as backstory. If you do include some of that history, it's probably best to leave it in the preface or even relegate it to a section in the back of the book in which you, the author, answer questions in interview form, a feature that appears in more and more books these days. Keep in mind, too, that all sorts of materials not necessary to the book itself can now be made available online as extra features to be downloaded for free or for a nominal fee.

Respect the experiences and vocabularies of the reader.

If you're a businessperson and you're writing for a more general market, then you'll have to limit how many stories and examples you provide that come out of the business environment. If you're not a parent but are working on a project that will include parents, then find some stories involving children. Respecting the reader's vocabulary and experience will usually broaden the scope of your work.

Choose vocabulary that will be the clearest and most compelling for your target audience. What this means for many spirituality writers is giving up religious terminology. We are truly in the post-Christian era here in the United States, and we cannot expect anyone to understand the vocabulary and terminology of a specific religious subculture. If certain terms are important to the book, then introduce and define them at the outset; assume that no readers understand what you're talking about unless you provide a clear explanation.

Use examples, illustrations, stories, and anecdotes that will welcome and include the target audience—even if these do not speak the most powerfully to you personally. I've noticed that many writers refer to times of retreat in beautiful, off-the-beaten-path places. One writer was able to spend three months traveling and writing her reflections. Another writer owns a cottage on Lake Superior. They are fortunate to have these experiences and situations, but many people do not have such luxuries. So, even if you're blessed to spend a month writing in a villa in Tuscany or an ocean-side cottage in Costa Rica, perhaps don't make that a focal point of your writing. In fact, does the reader need to know about your month in a villa? Can you write good material without making reference to it? Can you simply relate a scene involving you being outdoors when the autumn colors were high, or being in a place one night so remote you could see thousands of stars? If you feel that the particular details of this special locale are integral to your story, then relate them humbly and graciously. Remember, this writing is for the reader, not for you. And if I, the reader, have turned to your book out of some need, I may get discouraged, or envious, if the life experience you describe is not accessible to me. Yes, some writers can turn exotic experiences into bestsellers—think of *Eat, Pray, Love*—but if we write to help others spiritually, we are crafting stories not just to entertain or help readers escape but to help them dwell in their own lives more fully.

Create a structure (outline, progression) that assists the reader in following where you go.

Even a more free-flowing writing style needs a structure that enables the reader to follow where you go.

Don't assume that the reader starts where you are starting. You can't remind yourself often enough that the reader will not read your mind and have at his disposal your history of memories and information. Assume that the reader is ignorant and must be drawn into this topic and all its necessary specifics.

Don't avoid good organization because you prefer writing that's more intuitive and creative. When you're writing nonfiction, your readers will appreciate it if they don't have to keep paging back to figure out what's going on (actually, fiction readers appreciate this, too). They'll need some sense of chronology if you're writing memoir, whether or not you are writing the memoir in chronological order.

Keep it simple; each chapter should lead to the next chapter logically and should focus on one primary point, action, or idea. If the writing is intuitive and contemplative, it's still better to organize it so that the reader remains with one particular idea in one chapter. If the chapter theme holds steady, then the reader will be able to stay with you through various anecdotes and reflections. If you are trying to create an experience for the reader, then the experience will happen more easily if there is only one focal point at a time.

Remember that this is not about you.

When you take classes or complete degree programs in writing, it's expected that you'll show off how good you are at the craft. You can be original and clever and make sure people remember who you are by your style and attitude. But when you're writing for others—and when you write on spirituality, the assumption is that you're doing this for the benefit of readers—it's time to strip out the drama and attention-getting devices and put your reader first.

Your aim as a writer is to be clear and compelling. No matter how great you are at complex constructions, the reader should not have to read something multiple times to understand what you wrote. The reader should not be stopping midsentence or page or paragraph because he is awestruck at your writing. In fact, writing that draws attention to itself is usually drawing attention away from the content. When you write for others, you're doing your best to fade into the background so that the story itself can speak. You can be funny, creative, even mystical—I'm not saying that the writing must be predictable or boring. But sometimes we cross a line, especially if we're playing, mentally, to an audience of professors, writing peers, or literary critics we're still trying to impress. The need to impress dies hard in the writing life. But if a person is writing for the good of others, the need to impress must be overridden. Your aim now is not to impress readers with your skill but to seduce them into paying attention to their own lives.

At the same time, allow your passion and vision to infuse what you say, just as you would if you were sitting across the table from the reader. Taking yourself out of the limelight does not require that you cease to engage or entertain. Your engagement and passion are what attract the reader to this thought or scene. Be yourself, and allow that real person to show up in the writing. The reader should feel as if he's met a person, and this is even better if you are so genuine and generous that the reader likes hanging out with you. Give this encounter-through-words your best energy.

Consider that what you write is your side of a conversation with the reader. Be attentive and respectful. As you are writing, stop and listen to that imaginary reader. Learn to be quiet in order to converse well. Be willing to take suggestions. Sometimes it's good to have someone read your material as it develops; listen to the reviewer's concerns, questions, and suggestions. You won't apply each one, but those concerns, questions, and suggestions are the other side of the conversation, and you are foolish not to listen.

Work from the assumption that your book makes a promise to the reader.

The reader has your book in hand because she believes you have something to give her.

Be clear about what you expect the reader to gain from experiencing this book. Do this right up front, in the first pages of the book. In the first paragraphs. State why you think this book is necessary, what you think people need. Then state what this book will do to help fulfill that need.

Make sure you follow through on what you set out to do in the beginning. It helps to go back to that promise you made in the beginning, to see if that's what you're still doing four chapters in. Use your promise as a measuring stick, and periodically hold it up to the writing to see if you're doing what you said you'd do.

Write as if the reader is desperate to have what you're offering. Deliver high-quality material. Aim to inspire and encourage, and challenge the reader no matter how mundane the subject matter might be. For instance, I quickly wrote the early draft of this book. Then I had to go back and revisit every chapter, paragraph, and sentence to make certain I had respected you, the reader, enough to make this sentence dynamic, just for you. I want you to feel that you got your money's worth. I know that you don't have a lot of time to read and you don't have a lot of money to spend. If you honor me enough to buy this book and read it, I am obligated to do excellent work that will truly help you.

If you are writing spiritual memoir or creative nonfiction, much of what I've just written will not apply in the same way it applies to straight nonfiction writing. You will indicate what the reader will get from reading this, but you probably won't be as direct about it. Still, in the opening paragraphs, the reader needs to understand why it's important for him to read this book. What you write to grab his attention—that's your promise.

Create an experience for the reader.

The reader will remember, not words, but how she experienced them.

Don't shy away from the five senses. The world of traditional religious publishing has long been terrified of sensuality, and yet the books that reach people most effectively appeal to their physical, sensing selves. They tell stories in which physical life is revered and celebrated. They linger over how something smells or feels or tastes. They dare to describe with care what it feels like to fall in love or give birth or sit with the very sharp details of a person's dying. Use sensual details; honor the body's life in this world.

Take care not to disregard the emotional life. Gone are the days when it was okay to separate the human soul into segments such as physical, emotional, mental, and spiritual. Gone are the times of ignoring one aspect of being human while honoring another. Emotional appeal is just as important as sensual appeal. Your writing should make people *feel* something. Writing that deals with spirituality cannot allow the reader to dismiss how he feels as if emotion had no place in prayer or discernment or living well. In Western culture we have elevated reason far too much and tend to live primarily in our minds. Spiritually, this is not good for us. Why do you think there is so much emotional pornography in popular culture—the endless reality shows in which people are frightened, humiliated, angered, shamed, and rescued? In order to be emotional we feel we must go to melodramatic extremes. This same need for wholeness drives the religious fervor of fundamentalism and cult behavior. In writing for spiritual benefit, sometimes we must let go of our arguments and notice what our emotions are trying to tell us. And also give readers permission to do the same.

Appeal to the spiritual intuition of the reader by daring to be provocative and truthful. This means that you will risk causing discomfort in your reader. When we're pushed past our comfort, when we are jarred out of familiar thoughts and phrases, then we just might see life with fresh eyes. Then we just might finally get honest about ourselves. The spirit God put within us will recognize the truth of something and will say, somewhere deep inside the heart, yes. This is right. Yes. This is what is needed.

Demand something of the reader. Make the book challenging but in an inviting way. Be bold enough to make suggestions. You might write, midchapter, "Drop everything right now, including this book, and sit in silence for ten minutes. Notice what thoughts keep recurring, and ask yourself why this is so." Send readers on the hunt for stories, information, and inspiration. Urge them to compose questions of their own. Give them stuff to do—easy stuff and hard stuff.

Come up with ways for the reader to respond to the material. You can suggest actions to take or include questions for reflection and discussion. Also, you can construct the chapters so that questions, meditations, and opportunities to act are built in.

If you manage to transform your story into one that will truly help other people, then God bless you. And, thank you.

5

What Authenticity Is and Why It Matters

People who work in communications, such as television or book publishing, now say that authenticity is the new authority, or authenticity is the new cool. It's a shame that the word *authenticity* has now become overused and worn out, almost beyond having any meaning at all. It's a lovely word—it even *sounds* lovely. Its meaning is woven into concepts such as truth, realism, and integrity. *Authentic* means, "This is the real thing."

So, try to forget how often you've heard *authenticity* tossed around like so much marketing pizzazz. Let's explore what it isn't, and what it is.

Authenticity is not brutal and unedited honesty.

Describing in detail your sex life (or someone else's) or coming up with various strong and violent labels for people, places, or events—these are not acts of authenticity. They are acts of recklessness or cruelty, or shallow attempts at getting attention. Writing in blunt, confrontational prose is more likely an act of aggression than it is an act of authenticity.

All good writing has been edited. It has been revised so that it represents the truth of something—and I'm talking about truth that stands above personal bias or emotional reaction. In an essay or letter to the editor, I might write my misgivings and criticisms of a movie that related sexiness to violence in a way that did not ring true, at least for me. I can explain why I don't think it rang true. I can also mention that the subject matter tapped some of my own issues about violence in sexuality. That would be an authentic bit of writing because I'm describing the situation and giving it some context. If, however, I trash the movie and put down the director as a possible rapist and cite how many times a certain vile word turned up in the dialogue, I may claim that I'm being authentic, but really, I'm venting. I'm leaking emotional response minus the discipline of careful analysis.

Venting is not authentic—it's just venting. Venting has its purposes, but even the venting I enjoy most—that done through parody and satire on comedy programming on television—even those "vents" have been scripted and edited, probably multiple times. They are scripted to express intense emotion, but the editing process has proceeded from skill and reason.

Putting provocative labels on something is not authentic; it's laziness parading as thoughtful prose. It's so easy to affix labels to people or ideas or systems, and it's easy because a label halts any further thinking on a matter. If I call you an idiot, I don't have to try to understand what you're saying. Discussion and thought have ended. The more authentic path is to withhold labels and listen to what's being said and wrestle with it intelligently. There may be strong emotion in this process, but the emotion does not obliterate thought and interaction.

So, the opposite of labeling and shutting down debate is authentic exchange, which opens up a matter and allows it to stay open and confusing and troublesome. Authentic writing acknowledges that this matter is not simple, that it cannot be represented well with mere labels or blanket statements.

Authentic writing is honest, which means that it tells the fullest truth it knows.

No one person ever has a grasp on the full truth of anything. Every time I speak or write, I have automatically become inaccurate. But I can write in a way that acknowledges my limited knowledge of the truth. I can honestly explain what I think and why I think it. And if I'm truly authentic, I won't stop at what I think; I'll continue by delving into how I feel. Authenticity covers the range of a subject, respecting wisdom both of the head and of the heart.

Authentic writing rings true.

If the reader picks up one false note in the writing, she will tune it out—and before long, leave it altogether. For fiction writers, authenticity stands or falls on characterization; if I don't believe the character would really say or do what you're writing him to say or do, then I will begin to mistrust this story. Not only that, but I will not attach emotionally to the character because he seems fake.

Remember that the readers who count—the ones who buy the most books and who will engage with your writing—have excellent bullshit detectors.

Because authentic writing is truthful, it will upset someone eventually because the truth can be disturbing.

So, if you are writing authentically, your primary goal is not the reader's comfort. Authentic writing earns the reader's trust but is not guaranteed to make the reader feel better.

This should probably go without saying, but I will say it anyway: when you write truth that you know is difficult or disturbing, it's probably more effective—and in my opinion, more spiritually centered—to temper the truth with mercy. No need to write this difficult thing with a self-satisfied "So there!" attitude. That will merely build resistance in the reader. A gentle and merciful tone will make it more possible for the reader to receive the difficult truth.

Authenticity often prevents neat endings and quick answers.

If you honestly can't form an opinion on something yet, don't spin out something anyway and hope it sounds wise. If you have struggled and struggled and failed and failed, don't write as if you're on top of things. People will pick up the false notes. They'll get irritated when the words start sounding awkward and tinny.

Authenticity steps back until the viewpoint has expanded and the emotional tone is not neutral but is at least readable.

Readers can process only so much anger. They can manage only so much sorrow or nostalgia or sweetness. Readers feel that they can trust you as a writer when they recognize that you are aware of your own emotional reactions and that you take them into account. They want to know that you're sharing something with them, not yelling at them or whining in their direction. In other words, authenticity is a by-product of maturity.

Especially for those of us who are trying to write on spirituality, maturity nearly always precedes the written product. Often we become more mature as we do the writing, because authentic writing demands that we grow up. If we want the reader to move beyond mere venting and emotional reaction, then we have to be doing the same. We can't really write about it until we do it ourselves.

Authenticity allows real interaction between writer and reader.

It sweeps away the pretending and the posturing and makes it possible for two souls to meet on the page. It helps build trust between reader and writer. It makes a safe place for the reader to be honest as well.

Authenticity invites engagement.

People can engage with material only if they believe it. Especially if you are writing on spiritual themes, take care not to set up your readers to lie to themselves or to God. Refrain from lies yourself. Don't write anything you don't believe. Voice your doubts as well as your faith. Remind the other doubters out there that they are in good company and that doubting is not an unpardonable sin—that, in fact, doubting is a critical aspect of believing. Doubt will drive me to the source of my belief. When my life is shaken by unspeakable harm or sorrow, my doubt will—eventually—help me pray, *God, what is going on? Are you with me, or are you a fantasy?* This is prayer that comes from our truest place.

Authenticity is holistic rather than selective.

What I mean by that is, an authentic writer on spiritual themes does not pick out her good days and her high-faith watermarks and leave it at that. Certainly I will include a story about God meeting me during a time of despair. But I had better include as well the story of the two months during which I could not pray at all.

We will never know how many wonderful "spiritual" writers appear as they do simply because of the stories they chose not to tell. I suspect that many spirituality books are written at a peak in the author's life, when things are going well and when faith feels clear and true. They write about it beautifully, and it sells well, and then they begin to get speaking engagements, and then they're producing videos and signing three more book contracts. All of this based upon a brief season in which they experienced spiritual contentment or growth or success and wrote about it. This does not give a complete picture, and although the author is not trying to be deceptive, in presenting this mere snapshot as the whole reality, she is, in a way, dishonest and therefore falls short of authenticity.

We can't expect a writer to include everything—in fact, good writing and editing choose what not to say. But when the meaning of the whole story is altered because of what's been left unsaid, the telling is not quite true, it is amiss.

Not only does selective writing misrepresent you, the writer, but it skews the picture for the people who are reading you. It's sort of like how fashion models and movie stars skew reality for the rest of us. Their bodies are not the bodies of regular working people. They are paid to be beautiful. They hire people to help them stay slim and clear-skinned, to do their hair and makeup. They spend a fortune on clothes and submit themselves to hours of coaching by personal trainers who sculpt their physical forms. If they allow themselves to slip, they might find themselves out of work. I don't blame an actress for maintaining a perfect-looking body; that's her job. But when all I see in the media are "perfect" bodies, I can't help but see myself as imperfect and unattractive. Thus the movie and fashion industries have skewed our way of seeing ourselves.

In the same way, spirituality writers who represent themselves *only* as growing and full of faith and relating with God confidently—they set up the rest of us. When we read about those unobstructed "successful" spiritual journeys, we see ourselves as failures. Sometimes I think that certain spirituality writers have a following not because they encourage readers to embrace their own lives but because readers idolize the writers and want to become like them. Celebrity culture has invaded Christendom, just as it has every other arena.

If you want to be an authentic writer, learn to tell the truth, to wrestle with it, to reflect on it, and then to write about it with great care. And with greater humility. Don't do readers the disservice of selective reporting. When you tell the whole truth, readers may not idolize you, but they will trust you, and they'll probably stick with you because they have found in your voice reliable companionship for their own jagged path through life.

6

Spiritual Formation and the Writer's Discipline

Any creative act involves spiritual work—you can't get around that. You may not have a spiritual vocabulary or follow a specific belief system or participate in religious practices, but when you do truly creative work, you are tapping a place within that houses your spiritual faculties. This place is where you know the truth, where you tend your life in a purposeful way, and where you do the interior work many of us call prayer. This core does the sorting and synthesizing of experience and memory. It's also the seat of your morality and value systems. It's where your deepest desires live, and it is haunted by your most desperate fears.

So, to write anything of value is a harrowing task to undertake. Are you really prepared to enter the sanctum, to wrestle with that desiring, fearful, egotistic, wise, reflective, calculating, well-meaning entity called you? You must be willing to go there if you want to write anything worth reading, particularly if you are writing of matters overtly spiritual.

But here's the scary part. We have the capacity to form ideas *without* tapping that spiritual core. We have the capacity to speak or write quite persuasively, even if everything we're speaking or writing is drivel or, worse, untrue. Words provide a powerful medium by which we can make statements, devise theories, tell false stories, and form conclusions—all without the benefit of reflection or wisdom. Not only that, but now, thanks to the digital explosion, we have the ability to publish our many, many words and put them out there for anyone and everyone to read. We can be cruel, ignorant, misinformed, and lying through our teeth—and yet, there are our words, riding the cyberhighways and byways, making contact with other tender souls.

Every "spirituality writer" has at some time given words to the world before it was time. Every spirituality writer has written without sufficient thought or prayer or patience. We don't mean to write lightly or thoughtlessly or wrongly. But, my oh my, it happens. Sometimes it happens because we've turned writing into a business, and there's a deadline to meet. Sometimes it happens because our writing merely reflects our life, which has become careless and thoughtless and without reflection or prayer.

The writer of the New Testament book of James warned Christians not to hanker after positions of leadership, specifically of teaching positions, because the responsibility was great, and when a teacher made an error, it affected many people. The same is true for writers, and especially true for writers who broach the realm of spirituality. We hanker after those book contracts and speaking engagements. But should we be so eager? Do we realize, from day to day, the power we wield when we send our words out into the world?

Two disciplines make for a whole life.

If you want to write about spirituality, then prepare always to practice double disciplines. One discipline is the craft of writing; the other discipline is the intentional practice of spirituality. You are embarking upon two simultaneous formations, one of art and the other of spirit. Both formations are crucially necessary. And each can be practiced without the other, but both must be present when the subject of your art is spirituality. You can be a writer of great skill who does not deal directly with spiritual themes, and that's fine. You can be a spiritually well-formed and thriving person who does not write about the life you experience, and that's fine. However, if you write about the life of the spirit, then tend your own spirit well and develop your skill as a writer.

Spiritual formation and creative formation have a lot in common. I deal with this topic at length in *The Soul Tells a Story*, but here is a concise version that's a good start.

Both formations—of the spirit and of the art—involve some version of the following:

- attentiveness and awareness
- honest self-reflection
- consistent work
- help from others
- ample practices of engagement

Attentiveness and awareness

Paying attention is mostly what happens in good prayer and in good art. Noticing what's right in front of you; being mindful of this moment and place rather than allowing thoughts to wander off to the past or future; regularly taking the time and energy to look, listen, touch, taste, and smell. All of this is necessary for good writing, and it's also necessary for effective spiritual engagement. In fact, one of the benefits of bringing art and spiritual practice together is discovering how the physical senses and practical skills can enhance prayer—and also how a sense of the Eternal and Loving can open up deeper places in the art.

Honest self-reflection

Human beings are untidy collections of motives, hurts, memories, goals, fears, and so on. Much of the learning curve in any spiritual practice involves seeing ourselves honestly. Also, we must be willing to acknowledge all aspects of the self, including the parts that cause us pain, shame, or other harm. We cannot avoid the shadows and deep hurt. Neither can we dismiss those things about us that are quite lovely and amazing. A growing spiritual life leads to a growing healthy sense of self. As a Christian I grow spiritually by admitting what's not going well with me—and also by admitting that God's grace is already dealing with my sins and imperfections—as well as admitting that I am lovely and amazing by mere virtue of the fact that God of the universe loves me, creates me, desires me, and will never forsake me. If I am to grow spiritually, I will continue to hold all of that truth in grace-filled tension. I see the truth of myself, but that truth is complete only if it includes Divine Presence as an ongoing reality.

In much the same way, the artist cannot help but grapple with the many and often contradictory aspects of herself and of the work she's doing. She has to hold all things in tension and regularly train herself to look at the work as a whole, made up of who-knows-what. She also cannot avoid dealing with how she interacts with the work she's doing and how her complicated life interacts with that work.

Whether you're writing a short story or just getting through the week, things get messy. You cannot afford to ignore the mess. You can't live as if there's no mess, and you can't write as if there's no mess. Self-reflection is what you do to admit to the mess and work with it.

Consistent work

If writing is your gift, then write. Consider it your job. This project you're working on is the bit of world that you're holding in place for the rest of us. Your writing is your burden, your joy, your day-to-day time consumer. Figure out how to get it done. Work with your schedule until you manage to do the writing that's necessary. Write whether you feel like it or not—inspiration is the side-effect of sitting in front of that computer screen and typing. An artist doesn't wait for inspiration but generates inspiration through sheer work.

To do the work that needs to be done, you will spend your life negotiating schedules and day jobs and housework and childcare. You will fight every year for some retreat time that you need to prime the pump and feed your creativity. You will learn how to write in all kinds of weather, during various times of day and night, with people and noise around and in total solitude and quiet. For a while, maybe you'll write at the coffee shop. But that won't work forever, so then you'll write in the spare bedroom or at the kitchen table. You'll keep figuring out how to get the work done. Figuring it out is simply part of the work.

The same is true for spiritual work. I've never held the same prayer practice for more than a few weeks, if that long. So I just keep changing the practice and keep working at consistency. There was a time when I drove a car to work, and so my praying happened then. There have been weeks at a time when my best prayer happened on a crowded commuter train. I'm not happy with how difficult it is for me to be consistent. But I keep trying and figuring it out. I edit spirituality writers, and I do some writing, too, so giving up on my Christian practices is not an option. They may change and develop; some things stop working, so I shift to other things. But I keep going.

Help from others

If you're trying to write all alone, you're already in trouble. If you're trying to make the spiritual journey alone, you're already in trouble. It doesn't matter what kind of writing you do or what kind of spiritual path you're taking. Human beings are designed for community. I can say that confidently, even though I'm a classic introvert. It doesn't matter what your temperament is; one way or the other, you need help from beyond yourself.

Needing help presents a dilemma, because a lot of the actual work of writing must be done in solitude. A lot of the thinking and musing that happen while you're writing or preparing to write happens better in solitude. And a lot of the prayer and meditation that build the interior life happens when we're alone as well. However, the glory of this dilemma is how many options we have. Here are just a few resources for help, ways in which we tap the blessings of community:

- The works of good writers, filmmakers, visual artists, speakers, musicians, and mystics.

- Ordinary communities we're part of already: colleagues at the workplace, people in the faith community, family members, people we jog with or go shopping with, online communities such as friends through social media or people we connect with on a favorite blog.

- People we go to for specific kinds of help, such as pastors, mentors, spiritual directors, therapists, favorite grandmas or uncles, and life coaches.

- Organized communities such as writing groups, prayer circles, knitting circles, and hiking groups.

- Retreats and conferences of every sort imaginable.

- People we connect with on a personal level through e-mail or—remember these?—cards and letters.

We need help. Sometimes we need encouragement, and other times we need technical advice. We need company and a cup of tea, or we need several hours of focused work with someone else looking on. It is normal and healthy to need resources. Don't try to be self-sufficient; it will limit the quality of your work, and very easily such an attitude can lead to pride and defensiveness. Occasionally at a conference or workshop, a writer approaches me with questions about getting published, and I get an overly protective vibe from him. This is the person who worries about someone stealing his idea if his manuscript sits on an editor's desk for others to see. Not surprisingly, I learn that this person has never let anyone critique this manuscript. He's holding on tightly to his private world of words, and it's made him anxious. It also has prevented him from growing as a writer.

What assistance do you need? What support would help you do your work better? Try a few things and see what works. Get in touch with other writers and creative types, and be open to what you might gain from their company.

Ample practices of engagement

I really love how prayer can happen in so many different ways. If traditional prayers with words offer no sense of connection, then maybe centering prayer in complete silence will go better. If I'm tired of dealing with words at all, I can choose to pray with images or to pray by drawing or by walking a labyrinth. If I can't focus on my own, I can pray with others, informally or at a church service. If I'm feeling smothered, I can walk somewhere and breathe deeply, and that will be my prayer. The possibilities are endless. Any one form of prayer is simply a practice, and the more practices I have, the better.

The same is true of writing. Some days you need to write and write and not worry about how good it is—it's a time simply to generate raw material. Some days are research days. Other days are editing days. Still other days are for experimenting with language or form. There are so many practices that help a person engage with creative writing that there's always some way to do it. If one habit stops being effective, drop it and develop another. The more writing practices you have, the better.

Please remember, whether you're engaged in art or spirituality, it's creative work. And because it's creative, you have many, many ways to go about it.

Collect books and DVDs that offer a variety of practices. Here's a book that connects writing exercises with memory. Here's a DVD that helps you pray by chanting the psalms. Use it all—try out whatever appeals to you. These are practices. There is no one right way to do creative work. By their very nature, art and prayer invite you—compel you—to open up your soul to possibility and variety.

If Things Aren't Going Well

Sometimes, you know that you're not doing well. The writing may not be stuck, but it has ceased to tap anything deeper than your thesaurus. The prayer may not have stopped, but it has ceased to help you love your life. At such a time, one deficiency may be pointing you to the other abundance.

I once heard Madeleine L'Engle speak about writing. During the question-and-answer period at the end of her talk, someone asked if her faith had helped her write—or something to that effect. This happened years ago, so everything I'm writing now is my paraphrase. I do remember, though, Madeleine saying that quite the opposite was true. Every time she'd found herself wandering away from the faith, it was the writing that brought her back.

I believe that we are designed in such a way that our soul work—whether it's writing or praying—will always take us where we need to go. If we truly attend to the work, we'll be fine, even if we're struggling and nothing seems clear. So, when my spirituality is flat and loveless, I turn to the writing, and I simply write what I feel like writing. If it's attentive, creative writing, then more often than not, that creative work helps my soul come back to a place of spiritual calm and healing.

And when the writing can't find its footing and the block remains despite my efforts to write through it, I figure it's because my spirit is struggling or in pain or full of sorrow. Which means that the writing can wait while I go to the annual women's retreat at my church, or maybe I get more sleep and make a point to pray the psalms for a while. More often than not, as my spirit gets refreshed, the writing is freed up again.

To be honest, I have to say that I see little difference between writing and praying. They both happen in the same place—that core of my person where all the wisdom lives. They both require attentiveness and honesty and an open heart. And the two disciplines—the art and the spirituality—are so intertwined that it's really inaccurate to refer to them separately. When I tend to the one, the other is helped. When I dismiss either one, both suffer.

7

What You Can Learn from Other Spirituality Writers

The first thing you learn from other spirituality writers is that there is no formula that works for everybody. Spirituality writers are effective at what they do when they tap their truest selves and write under the guidance of the spirit using the practices that work best for them. Generally though, the writers who have had the greatest impact have certain things in common.

Writing and spirituality merge into one experience.

Whether you're reading Annie Dillard or Teresa of Ávila, it's clear that the author is engaged in her own spiritual journey, and that's where her material comes from. Annie's life is quite different from Teresa's, but there's the sense of an authentic story in both cases. If it were not for the personal journey, there would be nothing to write. The writers who move us most profoundly have, in their own lives, obliterated any lines between secular and sacred and treat life as a whole, in which each aspect is integrated with every other.

Truly spiritual writing is as individual as the author writing it.

If you really admire Annie Dillard or Teresa of Ávila, you will be tempted to try to write like her; this is natural and may be a necessary part of the creative process—you have to start somewhere. But eventually a writer has to allow her own voice to break through. This means that when you find yourself sounding like a favorite writer, your work is not yet done. In fact, you may have to start all over. The authentic stuff will issue from *your* spiritual experience and sensibility.

The difficulty with individuality is the writer's reluctance to put confidence in her own life as a source of spiritual wisdom and authority. Do you truly believe that you have anything worthwhile to say? If you do, you are fortunate—don't waste your good fortune, but write like crazy.

I went through a ten-year period of constant writing and publishing. Then life took some interesting turns, and my energy was required for other matters. Those other matters all but siphoned off every dribble of creative juice I had. When I was asked to write this book that you're reading now, my confidence was at a serious lull; I did not believe I had anything to say. As I'm writing this very sentence (months before you will have the opportunity to read it), I am writing in utter rebellion against my emotional state because I feel that whatever writing voice I had once has gone far away—I only hope it returns as I face the task of writing this. At this moment, it is the dead of winter, and I am bundled up on the bed with my laptop, the dog sleeping next to my tea tray on the other side of the bed. Every word I type here sounds wooden and useless to me. Fortunately, I have enough writing experience to believe—in a place that's deeper than the place that has no confidence—that there's a voice trying to emerge and say its piece.

It's probably no coincidence that I'm reading *Immortal Diamond* by Richard Rohr, in which he goes into much detail about the False Self and the True Self. The False Self constructs all sorts of layers of ego and angst and striving and foolishness, while the True Self, deep at the center of a person, waits for the time when the False Self will die and allow the real life to begin. Think of the False Voice as the voice you try very hard to manufacture because to you it sounds clever or deep or sexy and alluring. You write from that self, possibly for years, until finally that voice just fails miserably and sounds so boring and worthless that you strip away all its words. Sometimes the False Voice is the one that sounds the most certain or righteous. Sometimes it is merely your best imitation of the writers you love. What you can hope is that the False Voice will fail soon and disappoint you completely so that you can discard it and allow your True Voice to speak.

The truth must be told but need not include all information.

One of the loveliest books I've read in years is Isak Dinesen's *Out of Africa*, the memoir about her years of owning and running a coffee farm in Kenya. Years before I read the book, I saw the film starring Meryl Streep and Robert Redford. The film emphasized Dinesen's painful marriage (her husband was unfaithful and infected her with venereal disease) and her love affair with another man. The book, however, offered no details about her marriage, divorce, or love affair; it merely implied difficult times. Dinesen instead chose for her book the story of her relationships with the many natives who lived on her land and/or worked for her. She wrote of how the landscape affected her, about events involving illnesses and accidents, the various animals who became pets, or important meetings with tribesmen. She offered beautiful commentary on spiritual realities as she experienced them, both through her European Christianity and through her relationship with the Masai or the Muslim Somali natives she came to know and love. Hollywood needed to turn her story primarily into an exotic romance by filling in details of her relationships. But the author's self-editing served the book very well. As a reader I was curious at times about Dinesen's love life—after all, she was a woman running a plantation at a time when women rarely did such things. Also, I knew about her personal life because I'd seen the movie. But as a reader I was able to accept her silence about husband and lover because the story she told was so moving and beautifully done. And I believe she told the story she thought was most important to tell.

When Madeleine L'Engle wrote her nonfiction books about faith, she spoke as much of her doubts as she did of her beliefs. Yet she chose with care the details to include in a story. Trappist monk and writer Thomas Merton allowed his struggles to enter the themes of his writing. In his case, some self-editing was required by his superiors because he was a monk who had vowed obedience and whose work would reflect on his order and the church. The Catholic publisher I work for has, in a handful of cases, required a writer to delete some personal information from his or her book because of controversy or simply the lesser importance of that information. A writer might have to leave out some material for the sake of another person's privacy; she may leave out other material because it is not crucial to the theme of the chapter or book. Still, she manages to be truthful. She may not go into details of a divorce but will include that it happened and was devastating. He may not announce that he's gay but will write eloquently of what he has learned about the role of respect in sexual loving.

Not all accomplished spirituality writers are humble, but most of them are.

Lack of humility is but one spiritual failure out of many, and each of us fails in all kinds of ways. Every person has "besetting sins"—weaknesses that seem to trip her up regularly. So a writer who is gifted and honest and who cares dearly for her readers will still fail in her old familiar ways. Therefore it's possible that a powerful writer in the field of spirituality is egotistical and irritating in person. But ego so consistently gets in the way of truthful exploration and clear thinking that I think it's rare for a person whose written work helps many souls to be especially self-centered or arrogant. As an editor I have met just a few such writers. Humility really is necessary when you're delving into spirituality and trying to articulate it for others. You cannot be overcertain or dogmatic or coercive—these qualities simply mitigate writing that expresses love or hope or encouragement.

At the very least, pride will limit your effectiveness. Ultimately such an attitude leaks into the writing, and readers get put off by it and stop reading. Also, if you do the speaking circuit and are obnoxious in person, you will lose book sales for sure. I remember with some clarity attending a talk by a certain woman who was quite famous as a writer and a Christian leader. I'd had a lot of respect for her work, although theologically I didn't agree with her on some key points. But after I witnessed her sarcasm and arrogance from the podium, especially during the question-and-answer segment, I left certain that I would never buy another book by her, and I never have. Also—and this is significant from a marketing standpoint—I never again recommended her books to other readers.

What goes along with humility, of course, is openness and willingness to learn. And perhaps being teachable is for the writer the more crucial manifestation of humility. Humility opens the doors of your mind and heart, and that's when your own wisdom is refreshed by all the other wisdom that resides out in the world. Transcendence happens—and gives us something worthwhile to say—when we move out of ourselves.

Spiritual reality does not always organize well.

We do try to be organized and logical when we write about the spirit, but sometimes the best we can do is cling to a metaphor or two, such as Thérèse of Lisieux's little flower or John of the Cross's dark night of the soul. There's Teresa of Ávila's interior castle and Kathleen Norris's Dakota landscape. Sometimes what works best is a strong metaphor and good storytelling. Go ahead and try to put things down in good order, but if it doesn't work, don't push it. Just tell the story. If you like to garden, maybe you will talk of God in terms of death and gestation. If you are a musician, the musician's vocabulary might suit your story of spirit just fine. I once edited a book by a doctor who dealt with patients who had chronic pain, and so the spiritual story was told in terms of broken bodies and the longing to be healed.

If you are writing from your own life, then look for the major themes that have emerged over the years. You are a mother or a cancer survivor or a midwife or a chemist or a bus driver. Your hard lesson has been about forgiving a betrayal or finding your power as a woman or allowing vulnerability as a father or becoming a student of those who are poor. These are the powers that will organize your material, and they will form it better than would a standard outline. Most of the time, spirituality writing breaks down when put in a how-to format. Spiritual life goes far beyond how-to; simple structures of cause-and-effect and b-follows-a cannot support the truth you are singing.

This doesn't mean that order and logic are unnecessary; it does mean that the deeper truths may organize themselves by way of images, metaphors, and profound stories.

8

Simple Ways to Make Your Writing Better

I've led a number of workshops on the creative process and on the intersections between creativity and spirituality. At nearly every workshop, I end up including at least an hour or two on the nuts and bolts of good writing. All the process in the world won't help a writer if she doesn't know the basics of putting sentences together. So here's a chapter of boiled-down material and tools for the writer.

Accomplish these two goals, always.

Be as clear as possible.

The words must express exactly what you mean. You choose words with great care, trying out different options until you're satisfied. You write, then edit, write, then edit. Then you choose words again until they are precisely what you need.

Be as compelling as possible.

The reader must be seduced, unable to stop reading. This means that you get rid of a lot of filler. And you organize the writing so that it is intelligible rather than confusing. Sometimes you get rid of some of your favorite phrases for the sake of staying on point and sustaining the reader's interest.

Tend to the details of structure, tone, grammar, and word choice.

The following suggestions are listed because, as an editor and writer, I have had to apply them many times. Much of this is what I would call standard for the work of revision and editing.

Keep in mind, however, that this sort of left-brain, analytical work cannot happen until your generative, creative phase has cooled off. Many writers cannot generate material and edit it on the same day, or in some cases during the same week. If you find it difficult to do this kind of editing on your own work, it means one of two things: (1) you have not yet experienced the fact that revision is where most of the writing happens, or (2) you need to give yourself more time so that you have enough emotional objectivity to get down to the nitty-gritty of editing.

Some of these suggestions have been made in other chapters, but they are important enough to repeat here in list form. Any of these points can be elaborated upon by way of further reading; libraries and bookstores and online sources offer a wealth of information on the craft of writing.

Drop the introduction.

- Be interesting from the very first sentence; no warm-up allowed.

- Readers should feel that if they stop reading even for a moment, they'll miss something important.

- The beginning is usually not where you think it is. Most writers need some warm-up pages to get to the true beginning. What the writer needs to get started writing is rarely if ever what the reader needs to start reading.

Get personal.

- Readers need a body, a person they can walk with, whether in fiction or in nonfiction.

- Readers quickly sense dishonesty. Tell the truth, whether in fiction or in nonfiction.

- If readers can't relate to it or don't believe it, you've already lost them.
- Express what your experience is, not what you think it should be.

Don't write down to your audience.

- You can assume that people are ignorant of some things specific to your topic and take care to elaborate on those points, but don't write as if your readers are stupid. Don't make all the connections for them; let them do some of the work. Overexplaining something is a sure way to kill the writing.
- Sometimes a perfectly logical progression of thought and explanation becomes a form of spoon-feeding. Unless they're reading instruction manuals or looking up medical information, most people pick up books for more than the mere information. They want to be invited into an experience that holds their interest and feels stimulating.
- Readers get irritated and stop reading when the tone of the writing insults them—even if they haven't figured out what bothers them about the tone.

Include your audience.

- Suit the topic, tone, and style to the audience.

- Use the audience's vocabulary and common experiences. You have to consider gender, nationality, geographic region, age group, interest group, and so on.

- Speak from your own experience, but don't speak about yourself too much. Readers need to know enough about you to relate to you. Beyond that, they want the material to be about them, not about you.

Don't lecture.

- The more abstract you are, the sooner they'll forget what you wrote. Write beyond the ideas to stories and examples. Writers who use the Bible as a main resource are often guilty of writing in general spiritual terms and lofty theological ideas without grounding them in real experience or in story.

- The more you scold or give advice, the more readers will resist and stop reading.

- Every reader has a personal wall that you must climb over or get around. Writing that's judgmental and didactic doesn't work for this; writing that is gentle and honest just might.

Take the shorter route to the point.

- Life is short and people are busy. They don't have time for extra words.

- No turn of phrase is so brilliant or so sacred that it can't be deleted.

- Parenthetical statements often are unnecessary statements—or, if they are necessary, then they shouldn't be in parentheses in the first place.

- When using personal anecdotes, know that details important to you might be meaningless to the reader.

- Keep track of how many points you're making in a single paragraph, page, scene, or chapter. Consider paring down the number to one point. It's more difficult to get to the point if there are multiple points in a section.

Don't describe; evoke.

- When you provide too much description, you are dictating to your readers' imaginations. Imaginations do not like to take orders.

- You want to choose a few words that will stimulate the readers' imaginations so that each person can truly enter the situation and thought process.

- Choose words and phrases that are emotionally powerful. This is more important than choosing words and phrases that demonstrate your writing skills and extensive vocabulary.

For example: "Aunt Justine was my favorite relative because she never had her own plan for my life." Most readers will have experienced a controlling or overly eager relative, which means that this description of Aunt Justine makes them like her right away. Notice that in this instance I leave out physical details because the more important information is Aunt Justine's character.

Include sensory details.

- People live in bodies that function through physical, concrete senses. People respond to stories that resonate with their physical experience.

- Involve the whole person by including details that will engage the senses.

- Most writers favor one or two senses over the others. I may include many visual details but none about scents or textures. Appeal to the reader through all senses—not all of them all the time, but all of them ultimately throughout the work.

Not this: "Jesus arrived at the well around midday and met the woman. They struck up a conversation in which Jesus helped her understand that what she was experiencing was inner thirst." This tells the truth but without any sensual appeal.

Better: "We know what it's like to walk a lot farther than we'd planned, in the middle of a scorching July day, with no water fountain or vending machine in sight. When Jesus finally got to that well around noon, he needed to pull up some cool water and rest his burning feet. Who knows if he hoped to find some woman waiting to talk about theology? The first thing he connected with was her desperate thirst."

Use concrete, specific language.

Not this: "A mean old man lived next door."

More like this: "Mr. Adams was about a hundred years old, and he glared at us every time we came within five feet of his lawn."

Use adjectives and adverbs sparingly.

- Not only do they waste space, but they dictate too much to the reader.

- Don't let an adverb do what the right verb could do or has already done.

Not this: "It was a beautiful spring morning, with colorful birds singing exquisitely and delightful flowers dancing happily in the breeze." (four adjectives, two adverbs)

More like this: "In mid-April, the air filled with light by 7 a.m. A robin flashed his tummy and trilled at me from the oak near the driveway, and tulips, scattered across the grass like Easter eggs, quivered in a breeze I could barely feel." (This is still too long, but vivid without a single adjective or adverb.)

Use active, not passive, language.

- Passive language puts the important stuff too late in the sentence. The subject and the verb usually belong at the beginning of a sentence.

- Passive language uses verbs such as "is" and "was" in a static, rather than dynamic, way. If you want the reader to walk with you, the words have got to *move*.

Not this: "Mom, I was hit by him!"

Yes, this: "Mom, he hit me!"

Not this: "In academic writing, passive language is often used. Distance between the writer and the audience is created by passive language, but it has the characteristic of being flat emotionally. It is not desired by a writer to have distance between himself and the audience. It is much more desirable for an emotional connection to be made with the audience."

More like this: "Academic writers often use passive language because it is objective and impersonal. However, this creates distance between the writer and the audience, and even an academic writer needs to establish some emotional connection with the reader."

Develop an ear for clichés, jargon, and uninteresting language.

- Find new ways to describe familiar stories and concepts.

- If you are bored writing it, your audience will certainly be bored reading it.

- If you sound like one of your favorite writers, then rewrite until you don't.

- If you are using a term that's familiar to the audience, expect people to assume that they already know what you're going to say, which means they'll skip this paragraph and go to one that seems to have new information.

- From time to time, analyze sentence length and structure; writers often fall into patterns using a certain number of words or a particular sentence structure—for instance, ending each sentence with a dash and final clause.

- Every generation must learn the same lessons and explore the same truths, and we have to style the information in a way that communicates effectively to a specific audience at a specific time.

Learn to balance.

- Not just ideas, but also stories.
- Not just explanations, but also examples.
- Not just statements, but also questions.

Beware of your favorite tricks.

Every writer has favorite devices or tricks—I call these "author tics." Check your writing from time to time and make certain you're using a variety of ways to communicate.

- Do you tell stories without helping the audience make connections to the personal or spiritual implications? Or, do you overexplain those connections?
- Do you explain and theorize without providing concrete examples?
- Do you spend most of your time making statements?
- Do you insert a lot of parenthetical statements?
- Do you have favorite words or phrases that keep cropping up? If you suspect this, then do a global search and reassess in each case if this is the best word or phrase to use.
- Are you in love with flashbacks?
- Does your fiction neglect dialogue, or is it almost entirely dialogue?

- Are you overly fond of run-on sentences?

- Have you fallen into the habit of trying to manufacture drama by using too many one-sentence paragraphs, or exclamation points, or excessive italics? Usually when we must rely on such devices, we are trying to make up for weak writing.

In your own reading, put on an editorial hat occasionally. If you're really enjoying a book, figure out why. Do you enjoy the tone of it, the selection of descriptors? Do the sentences and paragraphs sing in your head? Take some notes about what strikes you—the technical reasons this writing appeals to you. As you notice what other writers are doing correctly, you can feed your own skills.

The opposite experiences will help, too. When you get irritated with a book enough to put it down, try to determine why you're irritated. Try to pinpoint what is exasperating about this reading experience and take some notes. Apply this information to your own work.

Indispensible Tools

For all the inspiration, spirituality writing is a skill that is learned, and any skill has its tools. This is not a comprehensive list, but it's enough to get you started.

Reference works on spelling, punctuation, grammar, style, and format

Most book publishers conform their publications to the *Chicago Manual of Style*, so any writer seeking work in that market should own a copy, study it, and know how to find whatever information she needs in it. Now that so much is available online, you don't need space for huge dictionaries, thesauruses, and grammar books, but you need them in some form.

Sources that provide accurate information about the particular faith tradition in which you are writing

You may not be writing theology, but it's important that you understand the theology of the audience for which you are writing. That means that if you write for the Catholic market, you need to be able to get around in the *Catechism of the Catholic Church*, and you need a working knowledge of everything that is important in that tradition. For instance, back when I worked in Protestant publishing companies, I knew very little about saints because saints are not part of Protestant traditions. Catholic, Eastern Orthodox, and Anglican traditions have a fairly robust relationship with the calendar of saints. So now I'm pretty handy with *Butler's Lives of the Saints* and other sources, and I know the difference between someone who has been beatified but not canonized.

If you write for a broader spirituality market, there's more you have to know. What is the difference between contemplation in the Buddhist tradition and that in the Jewish tradition? Does anyone still use the term New Age? In this instance, do you capitalize Orthodox or not?

Training opportunities for writing, editing, and copyediting

I never trained formally for the job I now perform because I was a music major, albeit a music major who had been writing since fourth grade and who took every creative writing course she could (how clueless is a young adult about her true desires?). Even though I earned a master's degree in print/journalism and learned much about writing and editing while doing coursework, I learned just about everything else on the job, starting out as an assistant editor who merely entered into the computer file the changes my senior editor made on hard copy. I did find opportunities to build my knowledge, such as short intensive courses or workshops at editorial conferences, and I attended writers' retreats and workshops as I could, but I'm still wistful about the thorough training in writing and editing that could have given me a firmer foundation earlier in my editing career—and that could have shored up my writing skills sooner.

Writing courses are available on physical campuses and online; if you're able to take advantage, go for it. Nothing like strong training in the basics to build the beauty of your writing.

Good examples of the work you want to do

If you want to be a great blogger, then find the blogs that are succeeding—that are providing quality material and pulling in a lot of readers. If your thing is magazine articles or devotional books or short stories or some form of how-to, find the best examples of those genres. In order to be a provider, you need to be a consumer. When you read strong books on mindfulness or social justice or spiritual memoir, you build the interior world from which you then will write. Also, you will absorb a lot of information merely by reading others' good work.

Feedback from reliable readers

For bloggers, posted comments can provide immediate feedback, and the smart writer will pay attention to what elicits reader response. Anyone writing for periodicals must listen to the editor, because the journal or magazine has a specific theme for a given issue and usually they assign freelance writers (that's you) features that have established formats and word lengths. The editor knows her publication's market and can help you write for it most effectively.

For book-length works, you cannot afford to wait until publication to learn how you could have done it better. For this writing, you need good reviewers. You need thoughtful readers who can be honest with you about what works or doesn't work. Even if your aim is to be provocative and challenging, it's important to know when you're pushing too much and losing the reader. Sometimes when we're trying to push the envelope, we are more inclined to be strident and preachy; a good reviewer will let us know that we've become annoying.

It's fine to have friends and family read your work, but do not depend on their reviews, because those people are too close to you. Line up a fellow writer or two or a literature professor who lives in the neighborhood or a reader recommended by publishing professionals. Be willing to pay a decent fee for a thorough review when you are far enough along in the writing process—it's not much help to pay for such assistance when you're still in early draft stage.

9

The Engineering of Creativity—Process, Prayer, and Practice

As much as we spiritual folks claim to have abandoned magical thinking in this, the twenty-first century, we do hope for magic. We await inspiration as we would look for the appearance of angels. In fact, inspiration is quite like an angel—materializing just when we need something wonderful to say, just when we long to write words that are earth-changing and for which we will be remembered long past our deaths.

We think of inspiration in this way because the experience of inspiration can feel downright miraculous, undeserved, angelic. When the writing works really well and comes really fast, it can seem that the Holy Spirit has overwhelmed us. While I spin out a certain soul-stirring paragraph, I could easily burst forth with the Magnificat, Mary's prayerful exclamation after being told that she, a virgin, would have a baby.

Is creativity a blessing for which we pray and wait? Or can we create creativity? Can we produce it on demand? Are we arrogant for thinking that a lovely creative act could start with us?

The miracle of creativity is that it is already within us. The angel dwells in these God-made human hearts. The holy moves in the nerve and synapse and hormone and instinct. We are *designed* to create. So, yes, creativity can start with me. I can work at it, engineer it, bring it about. I can even instruct others how to do so through a cheesy alliteration of Ps: Process, Prayer, and Practice.

It takes a process.

If you want to explore process thoroughly, then please read the pertinent chapters from *The Soul Tells a Story*. But here are important points to understand about the creative process.

Each person has her own process, and each creative work has its own process.

No two writers operate the same way, and no two works have the same evolution. You may attend a writer's conference at which a famous writer tells you exactly what you must do to be creative. But he or she is really describing his or her process, and it might not work for you. There's no one correct way to work creatively. The key to creative flourishing is discovering how you work best and then nurturing your gifts the way they want to be nurtured. For instance, your creativity needs a lot of quiet, or it does better wandering out among people on city streets. You write well at night, or some other time. Certain foods help you focus. You need X number of hours of sleep to be at your best. You work with music on—or not. It helps if you talk about your ideas—or talking may drain away all your energy and make it hard later to write down what you were talking about.

Your job is to figure out how your creative process works—and then work with it, not against it. Don't try to make your process conform to that of one of your favorite writers. Don't try to change your fundamental patterns because you'd just rather have other patterns.

And understand that every book is different. Every article is different. Every poem, essay, story, meditation, and collection of words for any purpose—each has its own flow and growth. Learn to respect what the work itself is trying to do.

You cannot control the process. So don't even try.

The creative process is a lot bigger and wiser than you are. Don't try to force your will on it. For instance, you may write fiction, and your idea about fiction writing is to start at the beginning and write to the end. But the process leads you back and forth and brings scenes into your mind completely out of chronological sequence. If you refuse to write anything that's out of sequence, then you will likely end up with a whopping case of writer's block. One key to understanding process is paying attention to where the energy is. If certain material bubbles up—if that's where the energy is—then just write it and worry later about where it will fit and why.

Maybe you're under contract and are writing to a deadline. It's possible to work creatively while having a deadline. A deadline is simply a form of structure. Creativity actually likes some structure. Say you have figured out that if you write ten pages a day, you will meet your deadline in three months. So you write ten pages every day. Some of those pages are wonderful, and some go almost immediately into the trash. But the creative process will use the time you're giving it; within those ten pages of writing, great things will begin to take shape. So, yes, you have imposed structure on the creative process. And, yes, the process is happy to work within the structure.

My mantra for years has been this: You cannot control the process, but you must master the craft.

The creative process is intertwined with other processes in your life, and there's nothing you can do about it.

When you're pregnant, every process in your life will shift in some way; don't be surprised if you have to adjust creative work other than the obvious creative work of making a baby. When you are sick or grieving, the process must adapt because you have other important work to do. When you're in therapy because of trauma or dramatic life changes, the creative process will weave in and out of the work you're doing in therapy. Just expect this.

Remember, though, that not only is all this stuff messing with your creative work, but it is also feeding your personal well of experience. That's the well that will provide material for your creative work. While you don't enjoy the disruption of process, you can still be grateful for the raw material that is your life.

The creative process can flow much easier when you have the skill to back it up.

Sometimes writer's block is a signal that you need to work on specific skills. You're blocked because you've gone as far as your skill level can take you. You can imagine in a general way what you're trying to do, but you're not accomplished enough to do it. Until you build the skills, the intuitive, fluid, rather crazy moods of creative flow will crash against the limits of your word crafting and leave you exhausted and frustrated.

Prayer is part of it.

I'm not talking primarily about "God, help me write this chapter" prayer, although those prayers pop up regularly, especially as deadlines approach. The real prayer is your own soul-tending. It's not the writing that needs prayer—it's you. You need to find the center that is still and strengthening. You need to deal with whatever issue is dogging you today, whether it's anxiety about your teenager or resistance to the topic you're trying to write. Prayer is attentiveness to your life and openness to the day and humility in the face of criticism and resolve in the moments of self-doubt.

Professional writers learn to compartmentalize their lives enough to write regardless of how they feel. Sometimes compartmentalization is needed and helpful. But too much compartmentalization allows you to avoid the very stuff you are meant to master. The fears and desires bubbling within you give energy to your creativity, so stifling all that turmoil will eventually stifle the work you're trying to do.

As a writer, you don't have the option of ignoring aspects of your life that need attention. Pray your way to peace or strength or comfort or knowledge. Allow the Divine to do its work in you; otherwise, what will you have to write about?

Practice leads to skill.

I have a couple of grammar books on my desk at work, and when I can, I browse through them and linger where I need to learn more. I have various other books that help me brush up on vocabulary and general knowledge. Although my full-time job is editing, I write regularly. Sometimes the only writing I do is for the work-related blog I host, but I am always writing something because my own skills have to stay sharp if I'm to help other writers.

My fiction writing has had a longer hiatus than I'd intended, so much so that I feel nervous approaching fiction again. So I bought a book of writing exercises designed to help me start tapping the deep stuff again. I'm going through this little book and doing nearly all the assignments, as though I were a beginning writer. I need the practice. A writer can always grow and write sharper and cleaner.

Anyone who wants to write for publication needs to be writing regularly, because you'll always need the practice. And practice will nearly always improve your skill. It has to be smart practice, though, practice that challenges your weaknesses and forces you to keep developing. If you're a prose writer, work on poetry or essays for a while. If you're a poet who specializes in sonnets, work in another form, or try crafting a magazine article, just to stretch and learn yet other ways to make words work for you.

And when you get an assignment, no matter how small it is, do it really well. If you're providing a devotional reading for a book or magazine, follow the directions given by the editor. Stay within the word count. Do your research. Make it shine. No assignment is too insignificant; every assignment can make you better at what you do.

10

Product Is the End Result

The three Ps—Process, Prayer, and Practice—will lead you to a fourth: Product. With any writing that you intend for a readership beyond your own small circle, you must, at some point, shift your thinking about the work. The piece might have begun as a prayer meditation, a Bible study, a journal entry, a class paper, a blog post, or text for a lecture. Now, however, you must see it as a publishable product, something with a perceived value for which people will pay.

You've gone through the creative process; you have worked with the material from the standpoint of personal spiritual experience as well as artistic craft. The final step is sometimes the most difficult, because sometimes, in order for a piece to become a product, you must add some things and take away others.

What determines the adding and subtracting? The market determines it. The company or individual who is helping pay the expenses of turning this piece commercial—that entity has a major say. If you contract with a traditional book publisher, this work is no longer yours alone; the publisher will spend tens of thousands of dollars adding value through editing and page design and will pay for publicity and marketing. Financially speaking, the publisher has a much larger stake in this project than you do.

If the material you've written is truly important to you, then you will need to allow its future to be somewhat open-ended. You imagine it as a memoir, but as a product it works better in the self-help or devotional category. You've put it together as a book, but the people most interested in it want it broken into individual articles for blogs or magazines. As creative nonfiction, it simply hasn't garnered the interest of a publisher, so you decide that you may as well rework it as fiction and take it in a slightly different direction; lo and behold, the publishers love it.

A *product* is seen as useful to a substantial segment of the public. You can write a history of the local community college, and everyone yawns, and all you sell are about a hundred self-published copies to alumni. You pick up a single strand of that history—two sisters whose restaurant served generations of students and faculty and who became famous for their fruit jams—and you discover a delightful story that catches the imaginations of people throughout the region, especially once you put together a cookbook of the recipes. Then you learn that one of the sisters eventually married a rodeo champion and traveled the circuit with him, putting up a pie-and-jam stand wherever he rode. Now you've captured the interest of foodies, folks from the region, and rodeo fans.

To create a product, you have to find the connection to the largest audience that reasonably can be expected. In the current book-buying environment, a story of vampires running a motel near an amusement park in Ohio will simply appeal to a larger audience than will the sisters with their restaurant and jams. The point is, know who will be interested in your material, and then work with the material so that it will be most pleasing to that audience.

The truth is, some of the most creative work we do happens when we explore the various ways of turning a work into a product. We daydream, make connections, imagine possibilities, and try various options. It's trial and error, but well worth it.

The book isn't the only product.

We're in the Internet age, and the revolution that has resulted is equal to what happened when Gutenberg invented the printing press. Communications took a tremendous leap. Information is now immediate, and communities form rapidly around events, opinions, and movements. This digital and cyber explosion will continue its impact on every aspect of human civilization.

For the writer, this is good news and not-so-good news.

The good news is that you don't have to obtain the support of a publishing company to publish your work.

Neither do you have to put up hundreds or thousands of dollars to self-publish, which used to be the case. If you are willing to publish only in digital format, which requires no printed material, you can turn your material into an e-book for relatively little cost.

The not-so-good news is that because you don't need a publisher to get your material out there, you will be tempted to publish without the added value of professional editing, design, marketing, and sales.

If you are accomplished at all as a writer, you know that this is a huge price to pay for immediate results. A good editor is gold; she'll prevent your making a fool of yourself, and she'll help bring out your best skills and wisdom. A good designer will help you produce a cover and other features that will not look like they are holdovers from twenty years ago. Sales and marketing professionals spend their careers learning to navigate the frighteningly rapid changes in the channels through which a writer becomes known and desired. No one person can keep up with all that. Effective publishers now have full-time positions to manage the use of social media alone.

If you choose to self-publish, the logistics and merits/drawbacks of which I will discuss later, then you owe it to yourself to hire professional people to help you build a product and sell it. This means that your upfront costs will be higher, but ultimately quality makes a difference in how readers see your work.

The good news is that you can write for various types of media and move beyond the book format.

You can publish in online magazines and journals; you can write for numerous blogs and even maintain one of your own. You can direct people to your writing through Facebook, Twitter, LinkedIn, Tumblr, and many other social media and reach more people than an expensive ad in a newspaper or magazine will reach.

The not-so-good news is that writing for a blog or online zine requires yet another set of standards.
What this means is that you have new skills to hone for these new formats and opportunities. Here's a short list of suggestions if you are blogging or doing other online writing.

- Online writing must be more concise and to the point than traditional print writing. Keep in mind that a lot of online readers are browsing one website after another, and they will click to go to the next page of your article only if they are highly motivated. So the important material needs to happen on the first page. You almost have to think like a newspaper journalist and make certain the most important information comes early in the article.

- Internet text reads essentially more like magazine and newspaper text than like traditional book text. Readers simply are not as tolerant of large blocks of text as they used to be. Even print books are designed now with more breaks in texts, more headings and design features so that readers do not face paragraph after paragraph of straight text. For people reading on the Web, bulleted lists and frequent headings are inviting because they are interesting visually and they help the readers synthesize the information.

- A catchy title and key words are essential if you want people to find this piece through common search engines. The advantage of this is that you put on your marketing cap even while you're composing the piece. Who are the people who will most want this information? Include indicators throughout the piece so that when those people search for articles, the words that are key to them are words imbedded in what you've written.

- Take advantage of links to related materials and other products you have to offer, such as a short video describing the situation that led to this article. You can link to other things you have written that don't even fit in this same topical category—if readers like you, they'll be willing to explore more of your work. You can also include links to your current favorite book or movie or blogger or website. People like getting connected, and if you help them find other like-minded people, they will love you even more.

Sometimes it's convenient to adapt a piece you've already written and turn it into a blog post or an online article. Unless you have already written the book material in an easily "chunked" format, you will have to revise for the sake of capturing your online audience. The writing must come in smaller segments and be pithier. It must be easy to grasp visually. For instance, if you adapt an excerpt from a book chapter or magazine article, consider adding some headings or, if appropriate, reformatting and trimming text so that it works as a bulleted list.

As the digital revolution continues, every communicator will be forced to reassess her written work for how effectively it will translate to new formats. How do you reframe a powerful meditation so that it delivers well on a smartphone? Now that any sort of written piece can appear on full-color readers, should you find photos and other visual add-ons to enhance what you used to say with words only?

11

Publishing Your Work

Of course, I am biased toward traditional publishing channels because I'm a publishing professional who works full-time for a publisher I believe to be one of the best in the business. Also, I have published various books through several other publishers, and I know that my work was helped greatly through those experiences. I believe that even though there are good options for self-publishing, if your book is a worthy candidate for publication, it's best if you have the support of a book publisher.

At the end of this chapter is a segment on self-publishing and when it's the better option, but for now, let's look into the reality of having a partner. . . .

The Author-Publisher Relationship: Three Stages

This is a general description of the publishing process, for which each publisher has its own version.

Stage One: Initial Interest, Communication, and Development

You have made contact with a publisher, and the publisher expresses an active interest. You passed along a proposal to an editor you met at a conference, or you submitted the proposal according to the guidelines provided on the company's website. Perhaps you had a personal connection and used that. Now that someone has read your material, he sees real possibilities. So the discussion begins.

In these early conversations, the publisher's point person—usually an acquisitions editor—will be looking for certain things.

- In what way are you qualified to write this book?
- What kind of person are you?
- How accomplished a writer are you?
- How willing are you to adapt and develop your material?
- Do you have any sort of platform that will help you sell this book?

In what way are you qualified to write this book? If there's a lot of theology in this book, then you'd better be a theologian or have significant training in the field. If you are proposing practical ways of running a church food pantry, then real experience is necessary. You need to have the authority to produce this book and expect people to believe you and try to follow your lead.

This doesn't always mean having a degree after your name. But know that if your topic requires any expertise, the editor will likely have it reviewed by a professional in that field. The publisher wants to be known for publishing reliable information, and in some cases there are liability issues. Don't be insulted when you are asked pointed questions about your qualifications.

What kind of person are you? This is particularly important when a person writes in the spirituality field. Some religious publishers require authors to sign agreements saying that they will, essentially, behave morally while under contract to the company. That sounds overcontrolling, but if a publisher is known for producing high-quality materials on, say, faith formation or family life, it cannot risk the loss of sales because a key author is caught up in scandal just weeks after the book comes out.

But this assessment of you as a person is much more subtle and complex than merely checking up on your public ethics. If I, the publisher, trust you to give direction and help to people spiritually, I need to know that you are fundamentally honest, that you are who you say you are, that you respect others and treat them kindly, and that your wisdom is proven in your life. I have known acquisitions editors to travel many miles and spend many hours with writers just to check them out and confirm that they were the people they claimed to be on paper.

Sometimes the writer may be a wonderful person and an honest person, but he is entangled in addiction or vicious divorce proceedings or treatment for mental illness. He may not be ready to write for publication because his life is still too fragile. In some cases, it would be wrong of a publisher to allow a writer to put himself on display before he is ready; that would be a disservice to the writer, to the publisher, and to the work. Certainly publishers know that some of the most profound wisdom and love are revealed in our brokenness; in fact, those are the stories we hunger to find and tell. We must take care, though, that the story is ready and the writer of it is in a stable place from which to write it.

How accomplished a writer are you? Most of the authors I've worked with have not been professional writers, and that does not surprise me. Many of our greatest soul helpers are pastors, teachers, counselors, spiritual directors, therapists, and men and women in religious orders. Their primary jobs might include writing, but that's not the main thing they do.

What we are after is the content of these lives. What we hope is that any given author can write reasonably well. Some helping professions require high skills in communication, and often those skills incorporate writing. With a little more work and a good editor, the pastor or counselor can do a fine job. Still, the publisher has to consider how much work it will take to turn the content into something that is not only readable but also compelling.

Some books (even some very influential books) are ghostwritten because the content provider either cannot write or is simply too busy to write. But in general, the publisher prefers that the author be able to do his own work. Most editors have lived through nightmare manuscripts in which major reconstruction had to be accomplished; some of us have rewritten so much of the content that it may as well have been ghostwritten. But we're not fond of those projects. For one thing, they take loads more time than a standard edit, and time is money.

One question I must answer whenever I review a manuscript that is under consideration for contract is, "What level of editing will need to be done to this?" If I'll need to do a particularly heavy edit, then we must decide if the potential sales of this book will be worth the extra time and effort. Publishers routinely turn down good book proposals because the authors could not write well enough. The quality of writing is a major consideration every time.

How willing are you to adapt and develop your material? The short version of this question is, Are you willing to be edited? If the editor reviews the manuscript and gets back to you with a list of things she wants you to change, are you going to become indignant and make life difficult for everyone involved? Can you enter a calm discussion about the ways in which the publisher would like you to develop the work further? Can you acknowledge that the publisher may understand the market better than you do? Are you capable of taking a fresh look at the work from a slightly different angle, one that might help you reach a broader audience or deepen the reading experience?

When you contract with a publisher, you have entered a collaborative process. If you cannot accept this, then you're not ready to enter the publishing arena. What you must keep in mind is that the publisher already likes your work; otherwise, you wouldn't have been offered a contract. The publisher already likes you. And the editor wants to help you shine and write a tremendously wonderful book. All these people are on your side. But it's on you to have the maturity to step back from the work and consider the questions and suggestions of the editor and publisher.

Very few books are so important that a publisher will put up with a contentious author. Such an author will make a bad reputation for herself and may find that door after door gets shut because of it. The publisher wants to know that this will be a pleasant and productive working relationship.

Do you have any sort of platform that will help you sell this book? You will always have a much better chance of landing a contract if you have significant ways to help market and sell the product. Are you a speaker or well-known teacher? Do you already have channels open to radio, television, or major news sources? Is your blog popular enough to generate a lot of traffic toward your book? Marketing never gets easy, and the more the author can help by using the connections and platforms she already has, the better.

Stage Two: Turning Your Work into a Published Work

After a point, stage two and stage three merge, but let's break them down for the sake of explanation.

- Developmental editing

- Line editing, copyediting, proofreading
- Design of interior and cover

Developmental editing

Much of this gets done during the acquisitions process. An acquisitions editor may work with an author for some time before the project gets the green light for a contract. The initial proposal is weak, but the editor sees promise and makes suggestions. The author works some more and sends the revision. Perhaps the editor and author work together on a better table of contents; perhaps the editor suggests one or two additional chapters that would round out the work.

Sometimes the development continues after the work has been contracted. When we refer to developmental editing, we mean that significant work must be done to the structure and sometimes to the tone of the writing before the material will be publishable. This goes beyond a standard edit and might mean that the manuscript goes back and forth between editor and author more than the usual one or two passes.

Line editing, copyediting, proofreading

Sometimes "line editing" is called "content editing"; both designate the word-by-word and line-by-line edit—what you might call the red-pencil work. The editor not only makes fixes to grammar, sentence structure, and other standard aspects of prose but also reads for the bigger picture. She is looking at how well the entire structure works. She's reading for sense and tone. This is the slogging part of editing, and it will bring the most discussion between editor and author. This is the stage in which the two of you solve problems and determine ways to make the writing stronger.

Copyediting generally refers to a technical reading of the manuscript in which the fine points of grammar, spelling, hyphenation, syntax, and format are checked. Sometimes the copyeditor is also the fact-checker, making certain that dates, proper names, titles of works cited, and footnotes are all in order. Sometimes the copyedit results in some additional questions to the author, but otherwise the author does not deal with this stage of the work because these sorts of corrections are non-negotiable anyway. For instance, the author can't choose to revise the way a bibliography is put together. Most publishers follow the *Chicago Manual of Style*, and an author will not override those standards unless there's a very good reason.

Proofreading happens after the content is "poured" into the interior design; at this point everyone sees what the text will truly look like on the page. Prior to this, an interior design has been chosen; out of courtesy, the publisher might allow the author to see this before the proofreading stage, but sometimes the author first sees the design when she is sent the poured pages for one last review. At that point, the editor urges her to look only for errors and to refrain from introducing changes that are not truly necessary. The proofreader is reviewing this same work, usually at the same time the author is, and is marking corrections for overlooked typos and word breaks, line breaks, and other matters tied to the layout. Any change made at this juncture will require reproofing and turns into unwanted expense.

Design of interior and cover

This happens during the editing process, and the author may or may not have much say in design decisions. It's astonishing how many good writers don't have good design sense; this is why very few book contracts give them veto power over cover design. It's common courtesy to show the author cover and interior mock-ups—certainly we want the author to be happy with these features. We listen to concerns and make adjustments. But the final decision lies usually with a combination of marketing and editorial opinion.

Stage Three: Marketing and Sales

Chances are, once you have signed a book contract, you will receive a packet of materials, and included in those will be a long questionnaire for you to fill out sooner rather than later.

These endless questions are designed to help marketing and sales staffs use every possible entry and connection you have to spread the word about your book. They want to know every periodical, blog, and website you can use, every published author or other expert who can endorse you, every group or event for which you might become a featured speaker, and every person who exists who can help build the buzz. These questionnaires require time and tedious digging through your files and address books, but this is the important next phase of your book's life.

Meet with the person in charge of marketing your book, and brainstorm about all the possibilities for promotion. Expect to carve out time during the next several months to set up signings and speaking engagements in key places. One of our authors was able to quit her full-time job and visit every bookstore in her state during the year after her book came out—and the sales figures testified to her diligence. Most authors won't have the luxury of quitting regular employment, but the few months after the book appears provide the window for any promotional activity you can muster. This includes using social media strategically—another task you'll need to understand and master.

A few words about social media

By the time I finish writing these paragraphs on social media, my words will be outdated. Which is the point. You cannot ignore the communications revolution going on all around you. You might still write longhand or on a typewriter—as you wish, whatever helps you get the writing done. But when it's time to get the word out about your book—or really, anything you've written—you can't ignore the growing collection of cybertools at your disposal.

As with any aspect of a well-lived life, your interaction with social media will ebb and flow, you'll have to learn new skills, you'll have to make choices, and you'll need to negotiate the amount of time you can spend on yet another writing-related task.

I did not subscribe to Facebook until my book *Days of Deepening Friendship* was released. I wasn't particularly excited about adding another time-sucking activity to an already busy day. But I wrote the book specifically for my employer's audience, and I was eager to help my company explore and experiment with social media in terms of book promotion and audience building. I confess that for the first couple of weeks on Facebook, I became an addict, checking constantly for updates and comments to my posts. What an experience—finding new friends who shared my interests and reconnecting with people I'd gone to high school with! After a time, I was able to ease up and use the tool without being owned by it. I subscribed to Twitter at the same time, and I have not been as avid a user of that tool; the idea of doling out my life's details is not appealing to me, but I have to remind myself that it's still a good channel for directing people to a website or a blog post or product page.

Blogging has worked well for me in some ways and not so well in others. With the publication of my third novel several years ago, I paid quite a bit of money for some faraway person to set up a website for me that included a blog page. The whole endeavor was intimidating, and I was slow to post regularly. I changed administrators and purchased software that enabled me to make more changes myself without having to pay hourly fees to other people—yet another process to learn. However, for a while I posted frequently and wrote interesting posts and had a few people following me. Then my publisher set up a new blog to track with the audience of *Days of Deepening Friendship*. This blog I write for on company time, and company professionals manage it; all I do is write and respond to comments. Because the administrative work is done by people who are really good at it, and because I write very consistently for it as part of my workday, this blog has had good success.

I tell my story to illustrate that social media has a learning curve. Since the days of my first blog, the blogging software has improved and blogging is much easier to do. Still, any social media involvement takes time and willpower. It requires consistency if you want to build a community around your work.

And—this is a significant factor for writers—blogging uses up creative juice. One reason I allowed my personal blog to stagnate was that I was trying to do other writing, and I was having trouble sustaining serious creative writing and an interesting blog at the same time.

Social media is here to stay, and it will keep evolving. A key advantage to using social media is that you can now find your primary audience and build a community around it. Today it is far more savvy (and less expensive) to capture an audience with consistent blog posts than it is to place a full-page ad in a magazine or newspaper. Whereas an author used to have to travel and appear to give talks and sign books, now there's the webinar, which allows many people to watch and interact with the author in real time through visual and audio connections.

These media cannot truly replace person-to-person interaction. I still prefer to travel to a retreat house, lead people in a two-day workshop, and sit at the dinner table with them than to connect through cyberspace. I plan to continue in-person contact as long as I am able to do it. However, social media make more interaction possible in more formats. In a good year I can make no more than ten personal appearances because I work full-time. In that same year I can make hundreds of other connections—direct connections—with readers and potential readers.

How many book sales result from a Facebook or Twitter campaign? The numbers are difficult to determine, and everyone in the communications industry is working hard to develop better strategies for optimizing social media. But we know for sure that sales increase when connections increase. Audiences gather when we show up, wherever we show up.

As traditional publishing models change and as social media become more prominent in the industry, it will become increasingly important for the author to be his own marketer. Marketing budgets are limited and must be stretched across a whole season of new releases. You are wise to learn all you can about promoting yourself and your book. This can feel uncomfortable for some of us, and it seems like not the best fit for a person who writes about the spiritual life because self-promotion is rarely at the heart of such work. However, consider this a modern form of the apostle Paul sending epistles far and wide. You can bet the man would have had a whopping Facebook page and would have dominated each new medium that cropped up.

The Editor-Author Relationship

After lengthy discussion with a room full of editors one year, I compiled two lists: one of "worst author" characteristics, and the other of "best author" characteristics. Here's a trimmed-down version.

The characteristics of "worst" author:

- Resistant to editing
- Not dependable when it comes to deadlines and other tasks he's asked to do
- Ego out of proportion to talent
- Tired message—not really fresh material
- Thinks that her manuscript is always the top priority on your desk
- He sees you (the editor) as getting in his way rather than helping to bring out his best work
- Is surrounded only by people who sing her praises, so the first real criticism she's heard in years is yours
- Ends up being someone other than who he presented himself to be, and you're stuck producing a book you really don't believe in anymore

- Must process every change, large or small, with you personally, usually on the phone
- Processes her every emotion immediately in your face

The characteristics of "best" author:

- Is willing to learn what the editorial process is and how best to participate in it
- Meets deadlines
- Talented and hardworking writer
- Worthwhile message
- Openness in general and honest in your discussions, even when there's disagreement
- Listens to and does his best to process your criticisms
- Argues with you when she really thinks she's right. Has thought-out reasons for wanting to go her own way in specific situations
- Enjoys brainstorming with you about ideas in the book and ways to organize and present them
- When he is irritated with you, he processes his emotions as much as he can before talking with you. He waits until he's calmed down before responding

- Respects the job you are obligated to do as an editor. Respects your editorial opinion, even though she doesn't always agree with you

There are two other lists, just as long, about best and worst editors, but this book is for writers, so I will spare you the long edition. The editor must be teachable, work well with others, truly care about her authors, enjoy a good debate when disagreement arises, give a real reason for every change she suggests, and do her damnedest to make this author's best work come forth. A good editor is an encourager, a coach, a technician, a problem solver, and in many cases, a friend in the endeavor. A good editor knows that although he may have the expertise to repair this manuscript and polish it, he does not have the life experience and knowledge to write it; the author is the key ingredient here, the one person in this equation we cannot do without.

Sometimes self-publishing is a viable option.

Until fairly recently, self-publishing was not considered a viable option for a writer who could produce high-quality material. If you wrote well enough, and if your content was meaningful, helpful, interesting, or timely, the assumption was that eventually your words would find their proper home.

People who went to "vanity presses" had to use that option because, well, they just weren't good enough writers to be considered by legitimate publishers.

It's not that vanity publishers were illegitimate, at least in the legal sense. They offered a service—for a price. Back in the day, I had poetry published by two such organizations. The fee for inclusion was the price of the books in which my work appeared. One book, which was full of many poems written by amateur poets such as myself, was lovely, hardcover, and impressive looking. Only after I perused the contents did I realize that my poetry had been "accepted" because probably no submissions were rejected. All were included, all paid for by their authors' purchase of the book. Essentially, I had paid the publisher to include my poem in the book. There was no vetting process and certainly no editing process. You would think that seeing my poem in this beautiful volume would have made me happy, but it was not a satisfying experience. After a few years, I threw away that lovely book because it provided no sense of accomplishment.

Like so many other aspects of the publishing industry, self-publishing has changed. Vanity publishers still exist; they continue to entice hungry, would-be authors to sure-fire publishing success for a fee. But self-publishing has expanded now, and for good reason: traditional publishing cannot accommodate the many types of book projects that are appropriate for certain markets.

I won't go into an analysis of the publishing industry because by the time this book is published, the information will have changed anyway. But a trend that shows no evidence of diminishing is the inability—and, more, the unwillingness—of the larger publishing houses to take on projects that have limited markets and sales potential. There was a time when you had your frontlist authors, your midlist authors, and a few authors that were high risk but showed enough promise or sheer gift or originality to be included in a company's lineup. In other words, there was room for risk taking, for trying out the up-and-comer.

Since those days, the book industry has gone through massive rearrangement; the huge chain stores put many of the smaller independents out of business—and then the chain stores went under, which shut down entire networks through which books were marketed and sold. Also, the Internet and digital publishing opened wide another arena that all of us in publishing are still trying to figure out. Taking risks on small-niche books does not trump the simple strategy of surviving and reconstructing profitable strategies for the new publishing environment.

So, if you have written a book that is well crafted but has a fairly limited market, self-publishing can be the smart way to go, especially if you are willing to do the project in digital format only. Print-on-demand technology does allow you to produce print books now without paying for thousand-plus print runs; publishers themselves are relying more on POD so that they don't have to carry large inventories. For the person who publishes her own work, POD means that she doesn't have to spend thousands of production dollars.

What you must remember about self-publishing, however, is that it does not—and should not—eliminate the collaboration with editors, designers, and marketers that adds so much value to a project in the publishing world. Consider these rules of thumb:

- Research any self-publishing company you are considering. Type questions about the company into two or three good search engines; go to websites for writers and editors and send your queries to people who might have knowledge of or experience with the company.

- If the company asks for your money up front, say good-bye. It continues to be the case that the publisher fronts the initial cost.

- Treat the contract with the same care you would if this agreement was with a major publishing company. Get an attorney or other qualified person to look it over for you. The attorney should be competent in dealing with intellectual property.

- Find out what kind of support you will get for editing, design, and marketing/sales. You should probably plan to do a lot of this yourself and hire freelancers to help you.

- A good self-publishing company for e-books will provide the expertise and technical support to convert files into digital format and place your book where it will live in cyberspace and where interested readers can find it easily.

- A good self-publishing company for print books will do the legwork for you; it's up to you to provide the book file, but the company's expertise is finding the best printer and getting the pages done and the book produced.

- If the company does not provide editing services (and it probably won't), pay a professional editor to work on your manuscript.

- If the company does not provide substantial services for design, marketing, and sales, look for professionals you can hire to help you.

You may need to self-publish if:

- Your story is too personal to reach a broad market but is meaningful to a modest-sized audience you already know exists.

- Your story is one of many about a particular topic. Yours may be well written but simply cannot find its place in the glut of other manuscripts similar to it.

- Your story, or its format or style, is too different for traditional publishers to take on. If it's experimental, a digital version that is marketed through cyberchannels may just work.

- Your story is important to you, your family, an organization, or other small and finite readership.

- Your published book has gone out of print and the rights are reverted to you, so you choose to make it available again, only in digital format. I am at this moment involved in such a process for my two out-of-print novels.

It's true that in a few cases, a writer has self-published, hit it big through social media channels and sold thousands of copies, and then been courted by a big publisher to sign on with them. But these are the exceptions. However you publish, you have to figure out how to sell the book—how to find the readers. And whether you go the traditional publishing or self-publishing route, you will need to take responsibility for getting the word out. The cyberworld is practically infinite, and marketing budgets are not. You have to find the best ways to reach the people for whom your book would be appealing and important.

12

Enduring Truths

What truths seem to be constant in the life of someone who writes for the spirituality market?

Trends come and go and are nearly impossible to predict.

The trouble with bestsellers is that they inspire hundreds of other similar books that will hit the market at least a year later, during which time the whole idea may have cooled off. It is possible to publish faster now—and if you write for periodicals, it's easier to hit the wave and try for it multiple times—but the public is fickle, and trends are called trends for a reason.

However, a trend helps the writer understand what the public feels it needs. It taps the collective consciousness of desire and fear. These basic desires and fears do not change over the centuries; our task as writers is to identify the many faces and situations of these desires and fears. How do I most helpfully love my adult son or daughter? The outward specifics may change from one era to another, but the foundational tensions and problems do not. No one will write another *Pilgrim at Tinker Creek* or *The Holy Longing*. The needs that made those books so popular, though, are still with us. The question is, What story can I tell that meets those needs now in a culturally resonant way?

Lulls happen, on personal and public fronts.

For a couple of years, I played a significant role in the life of a teenager who had lost her mother and who then was diagnosed with lymphoma. I had been writing steadily for about fifteen years, had published eleven books, and was well regarded as an editor in the religious publishing industry. But for two years, any real writing stopped because my energy was needed elsewhere. The writing that would have been most natural to do would have been all about the girl and the cancer and the situation, but I made a choice to guard her and her family's privacy, which meant that I did little personal writing at all. Those two years formed a major lull in my writing life. It would have been nice if that had not happened, but it did. My priorities were to help this girl fight her battle and get better (she has) and to continue delivering good work to my employer, which meant serving authors as an attentive editor. This vocation as editor also happened to be my family's main livelihood. Every writer dreams of being independently wealthy so that the day job can be abandoned for the sake of the creative work. But for most of us, this is not the reality.

Outside my personal life, the world—and particularly my country—was going through a crushing economic recession. Also, developments in digital technology were reinventing the publishing industry on practically a monthly basis. Every publisher, whether book, magazine, or newspaper, was fighting just to stay alive. People did not have disposable income. The retreat work that had provided extra income for me was no more because people could not justify spending money to go away and write for a weekend. All sorts of businesses went into a scary lull. One fortunate aspect of my industry—religious publishing—is that it appeals to people's spiritual needs, and during tough economic times, a lot of folks feel spiritually needy and are still willing to spend money on books that might help them.

We have no control over the various lulls that will happen at home and out in the world. You may have been on the verge of signing a book contract, only to have the publisher decide, while under mandate to drastically reduce production costs, that this particular line of products was dispensable. You may be moving into an intense time of spiritual discovery and journaling just when your mother has a stroke and must move to your home and be under your constant care. This is the life you have, not the one you've chosen. Your only choice is to accept it and stay open to possibilities you do not yet see.

If at all possible, keep writing during the lull. I gave up most of my personal writing during those two years of caregiving. But thanks to the *Days of Deepening Friendship* blog, I continued to write regularly for a specific audience. It wasn't the fiction writing I longed to do, but it kept me at my craft and maintained a connection to readers. When your life is in a significant lull and you are pressed on all sides by urgent circumstances, perhaps all you can do for a while is keep a journal or check in seriously to your chosen mode of social media. A recent bout of depression sent me to Facebook of all places. I could hardly drag myself through every day, so I decided to write, each day, a single FB post: "What I love about my life today." The depression has eased, but I received so many good responses to those posts that I've continued it. Who knows? That effort at self-care may evolve into something for others. It's not gorgeous writing, but it is real connection. Just knowing that a post has encouraged someone else gives me courage to keep posting and to keep paying attention to my life—and paying attention is the first and key ingredient to a meaningful writing life.

Resistance always means something.

If you have writer's block, dig into it. You are resisting something. Something is getting in the way of your creative work. Resistance always means something. Maybe it means you need to do more research; maybe it means you have hit a painful memory and need to process it; maybe it means that you're afraid to write something that others won't like. Or maybe it means that you stink at writing dialogue but you don't feel like expending the energy it will take to buckle down and study and improve that particular skill.

Part of your work as a writer, especially as a spirituality writer, is to do the interior work necessary to your own life. Resistance will visit you in so many ways—you will fight spiritual truth and emotional progress, you will run from relational conflicts and unpleasant responsibilities—that it's best to accept its fairly constant presence and deal with it as you can. Sure, you can write about mindfulness while your marriage falls apart, but eventually the marriage problems will demand action, and your writing will grow thin because emotionally you are spent and stuck.

It's not an option to ignore that inner conflict and hyperprotectiveness we call writer's block. Find out what you are trying to avoid. If you have to, get professional help. A therapist/spiritual director is essential for the writer.

It's really difficult to convince people that they need something.

Unless your reader truly feels that he needs the information or suggestions you provide, he will not hear you, no matter how articulate you are. This is where so many spirituality publishing ventures fail; we try to tell people what they need. Needs cannot be mandated; they must be felt.

For instance, a publisher produces a series of fine Bible studies. In the interest of educating people not merely about the books they love, such as the Gospel of Luke, the publisher hires writers to deliver on Old Testament prophets and New Testament epistles. People need a balanced Christianity! the publishing committee tells itself. They need to understand how the prophet Amos speaks to today's world. Well, sorry. What people want is the book of Psalms and the Gospel of Luke and—oh yes—the book of Revelation. Now the publisher has six or seven Old Testament studies, excellently written, that simply will not sell. And already under contract are wonderfully promising studies of Hebrews and James, which will not sell any better than Amos has.

In spirituality publishing, there is always the social justice dilemma. Every world religion has a strong tradition of working for justice and social welfare. In Catholic/Christian publishing, justice is high on our list of priorities in terms of ministry and community relationships. People in the pews need help integrating the theology of social justice into their daily lives. Writers are available who have been successfully active in social justice and who can write beautifully about it. But numerous publishers have provided such books only to see them gather dust in the warehouse. Social justice is a hard sell. Yes, we all need to get better at living in a socially conscious way, but no, we have only so much tolerance for reading about the world's suffering. This is a classic case of trying to sell people what they need and facing challenges to get across the great emotional divide. Ideally we don't want to be selfish people. When we buy books, however, we want those books to be about ourselves: *our* needs, not the world's needs.

All the writer can do is listen carefully to people and determine what needs they perceive and start with what they already feel and want. Once there, once the reader is with you, there's room to explore and stretch and challenge. You just can't start with the stretching and challenging. Rick Warren's *The Purpose Driven Church* posed significant challenges to its readers, but it started where the readers were—feeling that their church attendance had grown stale and meaningless. What Warren's ministry has done in terms of social justice is truly impressive. I think it succeeded because Warren is a true pastor who understands how to listen to the people he seeks to lead. He knew it would not work merely to urge them to action before they connected that growth to their personal longing for meaning.

Celebrity is double-edged.

Celebrity helps one writer make the huge speaker circuit and sell books by the boatload, and yet it prevents another writer, someone just as wise and gifted, from selling through his first printing. Celebrity is relentless and merciless, both for those who make it and for those who don't.

Does any writer *not* want to reach celebrity status, at least in terms of book sales if not public appearances? Let's consider what celebrity gives and what it demands.

- Celebrity gives you a great platform for promotion. People want to see you and hear what you have to say. They will buy every book you write, even the ones you wrote too quickly and therefore didn't craft as well.

They will follow your blog posts and tell their friends about you. They will share your link on Facebook and other social media.

- Celebrity is a way of the culture saying, "People *like* you!" On the bad days, it helps to know that. You have found your audience; you have this marvelous relationship with the public that feeds your work and encourages you.

- Celebrity is a great boon financially. Finally you can actually support yourself through writing because you are receiving royalty checks because the advance has been paid off and yet your book is still selling! Just be certain to learn how to manage your assets, or hire a professional to do it. A bestseller might tempt you to build your dream house. Sometimes what follows success is a dangerous bout of materialism, which is not always a good thing if you've become a trusted voice on spirituality.

- Celebrity can give you the space to grow and experiment. Now that you have an audience that is reasonably faithful to you, you are in a position to go further and take some of your readers with you. Because your audience trusts you, you can help their courage and spur them on to more growth and action. Celebrity has given you power—use it with great care.

- Celebrity can impose enormous pressure on your creative life. Now that you've delivered such an amazing book, it's reasonable for everyone to expect that you can pop out another one, and another one. This pressure can decimate your writing practice; instead of following the energy and doing the good work, you are constantly second-guessing, editing too quickly, and not allowing for gestation or proper development. At times, this anxiety will paralyze the most seasoned writer.

- Celebrity can make your life much more public than you want it to be. Unless you simply stop writing and appearing and speaking, your readers will follow you; they may even stalk you. This means that your life is even less your own than it was before. Depending on who is publishing you, what you say and do publicly might fall under serious scrutiny. For instance, you became famous by writing devotional, inspirational materials for women. Now your own journey is going further left into feminist theology, but your primary publisher is smack in the middle of the Bible Belt and its primary audience is quite conservative. Now you have a significant tension to address.

- Celebrity can make you forget why you love writing in the first place. Now your presence is pulled in many directions at once. Once you find an audience, you will become even more eager to please those readers, and eagerness to please can get in the way of going deeper, writing wider, and growing more honest and gutsy. You became a writer partly because of the profound spiritual experience it generated. Must you sacrifice inner exploration and hours of contemplative growth because now you are writing to three different deadlines?

- Celebrity can determine major decisions. This is especially true if you've made enough money to quit a day job, and if travel and public appearances have become requirements to keep your momentum going and your position secure. What does all this mean for family life and for personal retreat and development?

- Celebrity will tempt you to resent obscurity. I can't think of any major faith tradition that does not value humility and obscurity. Our spiritual mentors urge us to remain humble before God and the universe. Some of the most accomplished spiritual people let go of everything that celebrity values—fame, fortune, and power—so that they would be free to do the most important work. So, in a way, celebrity works against spiritual progress.

- In preventing obscurity, celebrity can rob you of some of the most valuable personal and creative growth. When no one knows who you are, you are free to meet the Divine and do the devastating work that is interior and beautiful and transcendent. If you don't have to care about what other people think, you are free to consider many possibilities. You might write three books that never see the light of day—but the writing itself has accomplished in you what all the money and prestige in the world could not have given you.

13

Self-Care for the Writer

The temperament that lends itself to writing and other artful work is often sensitive to begin with. You notice things that other people walk past. You cry over things that other people might consider ridiculous or unimportant. If you're not already a sensitive soul, then your creative work will develop that capacity because the work itself requires it. A writer has to notice things and feel deeply and cry easily and keep asking questions and hammer away until she finds the truth.

This makes for an exhausting life, even if you're a writer like me who is not athletic and who must work to stay physically active. The emotional and spiritual exertion that generates stories and memoir and other spiritually relevant material will take its toll on you, so you have to be sensible about taking care of yourself.

This topic really requires a book of its own, but I cannot in good conscience provide a writing manual without including some strong suggestions for the writer's self-care.

Stop apologizing for your personality.

You are one of those writers who can curl up with a laptop for days and hardly come up for air. You forget to return phone calls; loud parties agitate you, so friends have to drag you into social situations.

Or, you have moods that practically change weather patterns. You're writing this character who is going through a horrible experience, and you're right there with him. How can anyone expect you to just snap out of that and be all cheery by dinnertime?

Or,

- Friends and family wish you would just stop being so sensitive all the time. Every little thing bothers you.

- Once you get hold of an idea, you can't leave it alone. You're so obsessive!

- The family needs a whole separate budget to support your research on, what, one magazine article? Are you kidding?

- Couldn't you be a little more outgoing instead of being in your own head all the time?

- I thought you were a writer; why are you so boring to talk to?
- Why can't I read what you're working on? I'm just trying to show an interest.
- You'd rather stay home by yourself than go to your cousin's anniversary thing? What excuse should I give them—besides the writing, I mean?

Please remember this very important truth: The characteristics that make you seem weird, possibly unsociable, possibly unstable to other people, are the very traits that make it possible for you to see the world in such a way that you can bring it alive for others merely by using words.

Remember this, too: People who love you will learn to love your gifts.

When someone whose opinion counts brings a complaint against you, then listen carefully, because you may need to examine your life and make some changes. You may need to apologize or start listening more or keep better track of appointments. But when someone communicates that there's something wrong with your personality, give yourself permission to walk away.

Maintain reasonable control over your schedule.

For the rest of your life, everyone else will make demands on your time. You have to draw a line in the sand, plant your stake, name your price, state your terms. Someone else in the family can put dinner on the table, sort the mail, or wrangle the toddler. It's up to you to require that other people consider your writing a real task and an important aspect of your life. Negotiate for writing time the way you would reorganize to accommodate a part-time job. Respect for your various callings is simply one more facet of your spouse's love. And your children will learn valuable lessons as they watch you fight for the time and space to develop your gifts even as you love and care for them.

Give up balance as a goal.

The well-balanced life is a fiction. Some days you will give more energy to writing than to cleaning the house or listening to your best friend. Other days you will throw yourself into your family's needs or tackle a crisis at work, and your writing will receive minimum time and attention. You may go entire weeks of writing furiously and letting your social life languish. Then you'll drop creative work to help your thirteen-year-old pass history or to persevere with the soccer player through endless play-offs. Or, you could be in a season of life when writing has the front seat most of the time. The point is to allow for ebb and flow and not punish yourself when the schedule falls apart.

Plan activities that will restore and rejuvenate you.

At least twice a year I take a day to walk my city. Sometimes I walk the miles-long Chicago lakefront. Other times I explore a neighborhood or wander the nooks and crannies of Jackson Park on the southern end of the lakeshore. I do this because walking has always restored me, and I love this city that's always vibrating and changing. These daylong walks restore me in a way nothing else restores me. After I've had my day alone, walking Chicago, I come back a better person—a better editor at my job, a better wife to my husband, a better writer and homebody.

I've been saying this to writers for years: *spend regular time doing whatever fills you with wonder.* After you have written and written and rewritten, it can feel as if the internal resources have dried up. So prime the pump—go find what inspires and delights you. Sit in a spot that makes you want to worship and sing. Gaze at what astounds you; read about incredible acts of love and courage; work puzzles that bend your mind around; listen to the sounds that resonate and mesmerize you. Feed the art. Nourish the spirit. Nurture yourself.

Get professional help if you need it.

Creative work plunges deep into your life and stirs up all sorts of things hiding down there. At times, the turmoil is so great that you need help with it. When you've been writing intensely for weeks, one day you wake up and have no emotion left; you are flat-out depressed and can barely move. It's time to look up the number of a pastor or therapist or psychiatrist. There are occupational hazards to artistic endeavor, and the self-care budget should include office visits to the professionals who can address what's ailing you.

There's also the matter of spiritual delving, a topic not as recognized in the culture at large. Spiritual crisis is just as real as emotional or relational crisis. If you are writing on a topic that requires deep engagement with sacred texts, cosmic paradoxes, and chronic wounds of the soul, it would be wise to have a spiritual director who can keep you company when the going gets shaky. The mystics of various traditions have been quick to warn novices about the dangers of taking intense spiritual paths without mentors to guide and help. I'm convinced that creative work focusing on spirituality can in fact break through to mystical experience. I may be a pretty good writer, but I don't claim to know how to handle an unexpected mystical episode on my own. My response to a certain period of writing might require the help of a spiritual director or counselor.

For some spiritual traditions, evil is a reality that can become quite personal and malicious. As a Christian, I don't think it's a far-fetched idea that an intelligent force bent on causing human suffering might try to interfere with creative work that endeavors to help people spiritually. A writer doing holy work might encounter resistance because the task places her in a spiritual battle of sorts. So it's perfectly reasonable to ask for assistance in the form of spiritual counseling and others' prayers.

Don't neglect your physical health.

This is the segment I hesitate to write because I'm still not very good at this part. I work at a desk all week; I do my own writing with my back supported and my feet up. Physical limitations, such as arthritis in key areas of my frame, prevent rigorous exercise. Still, I know that my mind works better when my body is in better shape. The wrong diet makes me sluggish. Bad sleep patterns disrupt practices both artistic and spiritual. The right level of physical activity elevates the chemicals in my system that make me less prone to depression.

Sometimes a ten-minute walk will free up the tangle of sentences I've been wrestling with for an hour, hunched over my computer.

Do physical activity that you enjoy and that helps you. Train for a marathon or learn some gentle tai chi moves. Begin simply by stretching some in the morning and cutting out sugar before bedtime. You have the capacity to care for your body, and you owe it to yourself to do that. Also, the creative work you do will flow more easily when your body is healthier and happier.

Give yourself at least one retreat per year, more if possible.

Moving yourself to a different location can be just enough of a shift to jar loose the inspiration you've been trying to muster. All those bits of your daily life—the endless laundry, the layers of bills and correspondence, the wall that must be repaired and repainted, the pet that needs you every half hour, the drop in your kid's algebra grade, the friend's family troubles or the spouse's scheme for vacation—those things have less pull when you are nowhere near them. And when you have a place and the time to take a leisurely walk and do nothing but breathe and swing your arms, you will discover that you really *need* this, have needed it for a long time.

You may have become an expert at writing for a half hour here, an hour there, around the other obligations of your life. But there are times when the creative work will not move forward until you can give it a large chunk of time with no interruptions other than breaks for food, drink, sleep, and the bathroom. A personal writing retreat can give you this opportunity.

Be careful, though, to determine the focus of this particular retreat ahead of time so that you don't overload it. Take one writing project, not four. Allow time for extra sleep. Plan something fun or relaxing after you've put in several hours of work. Don't turn it into a social time, no matter how many good friends live within a ten-minute drive and would love to have lunch with you. Or if you must have that lunch, don't let it drag you away from your focus.

Perhaps you need a spiritual retreat more than a writing retreat. You want extended time for prayer and silence, with a director or alone. Try to schedule one retreat for prayer and quiet and another for writing work. Pay attention to what you need.

The location of your retreat will have an impact on the quality of your time. When I retreat to write, I try to stay in a comfortable hotel that gives me easy access to good food and places to walk. For a prayer retreat, I might find a religious retreat house where I won't be tempted by a television remote. The purpose of the retreat will determine the environment I need—how many distractions or luxuries, how noisy or quiet.

Find the community you need.

Each writer has to discover for herself what community means to her and where she will find it. This is the community that will support your writing life. One writer does best when she's in a writers' group that meets regularly for critique and encouragement; another writer does pretty well on her own but gladly pays an editor in her neighborhood to do a thorough review when the work is in a later stage. This author has two friends in his faith community who cheer him on and sometimes read and comment on his work; this other author lives in a tiny town where hardly anybody is interested in his subject matter, but he checks in twice a week with another writer halfway across the country, someone he met on Facebook months ago who has turned out to be a perfect companion on the writing trail.

A writer might find just the right community in the pew next to her. Then again, her writing life might have compelled her away from the church of her youth; now she lives in a city, and the people she connects with share the stage with her at open-mike readings every other Thursday at a nearby coffee shop.

You may long for a community that does not exist, at least not now. The important thing is to receive with gratitude the community you have wherever you find it. If you don't have the companionship you want for this artistic life, then keep looking. In the meantime, enjoy the company of people through the books they have published, the films they have made, or the songs they have recorded. Get acquainted with writers long dead through their published letters or through others' biographies of them. If you feel so inclined, correspond with a living writer whose works have helped you—it's not unusual for such a writer to respond to personal letters and e-mails.

Allow your spiritual life to uphold your creative life.

You write about the spiritual life, so do not hesitate to incorporate your spirituality into every aspect of your writing, including self-care. Prayer, meditation, silence, time lingering with sacred texts, slow reading, contemplative movement—if these help with your life in general, then certainly they can help with your writing in particular.

14

So, Where Is God in All This?

If we possess the barest belief in a Divine Good, in a power that has generated the universe and continues to hold everything together, we shouldn't have to strain to believe that this creative presence holds together the individual human personality. The Divine impulse drives our curiosity and tenacity and innovation.

Do you believe that your mere existence is a miracle? Do you contemplate all that must take place—on levels physiological, psychological, spiritual, and cosmic—for you to have a thought and write it down?

If you have paid the least bit of attention to your life, if you have opened your eyes and heart and mind to the miracles pulsing all around you at every moment, then you understand how ridiculous it is to say that God "inspired" this story you've written. As if God's role was to shoot an idea straight from heaven into your head! God was involved long before you recognized an inspiration, and God stays involved even when you are clueless about it.

The simple answer to the question "Where is God in all this?" is, "Everywhere." But I will belabor the point and break it down because it is so easy to think of God's involvement in our creativity as so many moments of cause-and-effect or prayer-and-answer. If we considered that Divine power is at work in us at every moment, we might actually own our God-given power to create wonder and change the world. It's easier to think of writing as a haphazard collection of dispatches from above, only a few of which develop into what they're supposed to be. It's easier to think of our creative success, or lack of it, as attached to God's blessing us for doing things perfectly or withholding blessing (and success) because we just didn't work hard enough or get the instructions right.

If we think in terms of God sending us inspiration as though it were an object given to us—or withheld from us—we tend to see the inspiration as a finite thing that is already completed when it arrives. In practical terms, this means that I am inspired to write a poem; it comes so quickly that I can barely get the words down fast enough. I feel that this came straight from the Holy Spirit, that its power rocked me to the bottom of my soul.

So, now that it's written down, I can't imagine doing anything to it because, you see, it was *inspired*. A gift from God that I dare not tamper with. This might sound silly, but I have received a lot of manuscripts whose authors felt that they had received the gift as a whole and that because it was inspired, it would be insulting to God to try to improve it. I do understand this feeling. Sometimes a period of writing is so white-hot, so unnerving in its truth and beauty, that I really need to leave it alone for a while. I need to let the words sear me and speak to me.

I believe that such a work is indeed inspired. God is present in it. But God is also present in my writing gift, in my ability to work with material. Think of it this way. If you give birth to a baby, you know that this is a holy gift, perfect just as she arrives to you. But is she finished? Is there no more work to do? You will spend years and years helping God perfect this already perfect child. It's your job to keep working on her, helping her form well and become the healthiest, happiest version of herself she can be.

When I write a page so powerful that it seems to catch flame, I can and should receive it as inspired, as a holy gift. Then, when the time is right, it's my job to keep working with this holy, raw material, to shape it until it has found its best form.

God is in the inspiration. But that's just the beginning. Here is a grand-finale bullet list of where you might notice the Divine in your writing life. God was/is present:

- in your desire to learn, in your unflagging curiosity
- when the light comes on and you are compelled to record what you see
- in the golden childhood hours when Mom or Dad read to you, one story after another
- when the teacher or relative pointed out that you're a good storyteller or that you write well
- in the family tragedy that forced you to go deeper for a sense of good purpose in the world
- when you failed at that job or project or relationship—failure that taught you about yourself
- in the numerous incidents through childhood and adolescence that shaped you
- when you first got the idea for this story or book or article or poem
- in the specific set of traits and memories that make you who you are

- when you connected with the right person to discuss this project's possibilities
- in the courses you took that helped you organize, write, analyze, and solve problems
- when you wrote those obscure articles for the even more obscure publication, for almost no money at all
- in the various jobs and responsibilities you assumed had nothing to do with the real work of your life
- when the best plans got thwarted and the detour turned out to be the real journey
- in every blessed revision you've gone through with this work
- when you faced writer's block and got through it
- in the critique that forced you to rethink this piece and try again
- when you got sick of this whole writing thing and left it for a while
- in all the books, films, people, poems, and events that kept your writing impulse alive
- when you must bear witness, reveal the truth, give words of courage and help
- in those eternal moments when you feel in every particle the reality of love, redemption, forgiveness, peace

- when you wrote so many mediocre paragraphs—which brought you finally to the really wonderful ones
- in the expertise of other writers, editors, readers, bloggers, and teachers who have helped you
- when you knew that this work was important, that you couldn't *not* write it
- in all the hot-and-cold phases of writing and revising
- when you finished, and rested
- when a whole new phase of understanding took you through yet another revision
- when you discovered the next thing to write about and started the process all over again

Your writing life is, simply, *your life*. The Divine is not involved in bits and pieces of you but moves and struggles within every aspect of who you are. The Holy is hard at work even when you're not; it is forward-looking when you want to quit. When you are weary of yourself and loathe your attempts at giftedness, God sees you already fully formed and your work accomplished in all its beauty and glory.

Now That You've Found Your Spiritual Writing Voice . . .

What to do now? If you have worked your way through this book, then probably you have the somewhat disappointing sense that there is still more work to do. You have learned as much—maybe more—about what *not* to do than about what to do. If you came to this book with a manuscript in process, you may feel that there's too much about it that must be fixed or reworked. Or you feel hemmed in and no longer free simply to tell your story because now you must think about the audience and what your platform is and how to market yourself.

So, in a way, I have spent pages telling you the many ways a manuscript can go wrong. I've spoken from my experience and instincts as an editor. However, my experience and instincts as a writer tell me that if you truly have something to write, you will write it, one way or another. You will read a book such as this one and stew around for a while and move through various stages of anger and doubt about your skill level and marketability.

But then the words will keep coming anyway, and you will get back to the honest work of writing what your soul is learning. A person called to write simply cannot stop writing, even if an editor sloshes cold water all over her manuscript and her dreams. If your spiritual reality expresses itself through written words, you cannot deny its expression. You will find a way to keep at it.

A lot of the crafting that transforms a personal story into a story for others, that prepares the story for a broader, more public audience—this crafting can be applied only after the early, personal stages of writing have been fulfilled. If you are struggling too much with the transition from the very personal story to a more universal version of it, that's one indication that you have more personal work to do with it. Perhaps you should turn loose your vision of it as published and public and tend to it a while longer as the intimate writing it is and needs to be for now.

Healthy spiritual delving through the written word can be hindered if the writer exposes it too early to editorial assessment. You may have a good work happening; then you show it to an editor, who has only this rough version to go on and who takes the idea in a slightly different direction that seems more marketable to her, so you dismantle the idea that was forming and try to turn it into something else, only to find that this messes up the creative impulse entirely. Spiritual writing in its earlier stages must be protected; consider it intimate prayer, and be that attentive and reverent toward it.

And sometimes, the story that is painfully honest and personal and painstaking—sometimes that is the most powerful version for the public. Sometimes the editor will come back to you and say, "You're still at the surface of this thing—what's really happening? Be honest, now." Sometimes it takes an editor or other reader to call you out and demand that you take the writing a level deeper and truer. Sometimes the real story is the one you still cannot face, and it takes another reader to see that.

All I can leave you with, really, is the exhortation to tend your own soul with great care. Allow it to tell you what the next step should be—for your writing as for your whole life. Allow your writing to inform your living, and vice versa. Consider it all the same. It's all gift.

Acknowledgments

Thanks to friend and publishing colleague Joe Durepos for convincing me to write this book. He saw the wisdom and necessity of it when I didn't. Thanks to every writer I've edited during this fairly long career; not only did I get to work with your material, but I was also privileged to learn from you, the expert in your specific field of knowledge and experience. Also, I've enjoyed getting to know some of you on a long-term basis as friends and fellow word crafters. Thanks to Loyola Press for making a good home for my gifts, a place where I could nurture my skills and participate in ministry. Thanks to my various bosses and mentors: Ramona Tucker, Stephen Board, Joan Guest, Dan Elliott, Lynn Vanderzalm, LaVonne Neff, Phyllis Tickle, Terry Locke, and Steve Connor. I will not attempt to list the many editors, writers, designers, salespeople, and marketers who have made and continue to make my working days sane and effective. Thanks to ~~scores of~~ workshop participants and the many good souls in the online community of the Days of Deepening Friendship blog—your feedback keeps me grounded and inspired. Thanks to my husband, Jim, who keeps our home steady and warm so that I can spend my days adventuring with words.

About the Author

Vinita Hampton Wright is a Loyola Press editor and writer of many books, including *Days of Deepening Friendship* and *Simple Acts of Moving Forward*, and she blogs for DeepeningFriendship.com. She has been practicing Ignatian spirituality for a decade and writing about it for nearly as long. She lives in Chicago, IL, with her husband, one dog, and two cats.

LANDMARK COLLECTOR'S I

HISTORIC
FAIRGROUND SCENES

Michael E. Ware

Dominating the skyline at this Banbury Fair is the Big Wheel. With the coming of the traction engine, electricity became available to the showman to light up his ride. Owners of Big Wheels took advantage of this to plaster lights all over them. Big Wheels then became a blaze of light in the sky and were usually placed near the edge of a fair to act as a beacon to attract the crowds. This photograph, taken at the turn of the century, shows a Wheel before it was covered in electric light bulbs. One of the snags of a Wheel is that each of the suspended chairs has to be loaded and unloaded singly. This takes time, with the result that the Big Wheels are unlikely to take as much money per hour as say, a set of Gallopers or Dodgems. The lady in the bottom left-hand corner is dressed in the typical costume of an Oxfordshire traveller.

LANDMARK COLLECTOR'S LIBRARY

HISTORIC
FAIRGROUND SCENES

Michael E. Ware

Landmark Publishing

Published by

Ashbourne Hall, Cokayne Ave
Ashbourne, Derbyshire DE6 1EJ England
Tel: (01335) 347349 Fax: (01335) 347303
e-mail: landmark@clara.net
web site: www.landmarkpublishing.co.uk

Landmarks 1st edition

ISBN: 1-84306-182-1

British Library Cataloguing in Publication Data: a catalogue
record for this book is available from the British Library.

Printed by Cromwell Press, Trowbridge, Wiltshire

Cover by James Allsopp

Contents

Acknowledgements

There is a wealth of photographs of fairground subjects in private and public collections throughout the country. For some strange reason the quality of these photographs is usually very poor indeed, and many excellent subjects have had to be rejected due to the fact that they will just not reproduce in a book such as this. I must have considered over 10,000 photographs in order to select the hundred and twenty or so which appear in these pages, and to those many people who have let me browse for hours through their collections, only to find I have used only one or two, I would like to say a special thank you. I have consulted many Public Libraries and Museums, finding the staff very helpful indeed. I would like to single out the great help given to me by Jack Wilkinson, known to many as the 'Cyclist' in *World's Fair*. Jack spent many hours reading my captions and then adding his own comments. In some cases these were so detailed that it was quite impossible to incorporate all the information given.

To my friend and near neighbour Arthur Hosey who spent most of his life with Arnold Brothers' fair must go a sincere vote of thanks for allowing me the full use of his collection of photographs and for providing me with so much background information. He too added a great number of facts to my researched material. I am pleased to say that Arthur is still closely connected with preservation, and attends many traction engine rallies each year with his caravan displaying several hundred of his fairground photographs. Much information has been gleaned from the large library of books on both the circus and the fair owned by John Pocock of Berwick St John, who kindly lent me all these for well over a year. Lesley Harnett typed dozens of letters and the manuscript while Michael Sedgwick read the manuscript and proofs and gave much advice.

The author and publisher are grateful to the following for the use of illustrations:
Banbury Library: *frontis*; Author's Collection: 1, 10, 98, 101, 102; South Tyneside Public Library: 2, 36; Benjamin Stone Collection, Birmingham City Library: 3, 12, 49, 50; Radio Times Hulton Picture Library: 4, 5, 7, 11, 13, 23, 37, 51, 52, 62, 64, 67, 74, 76, 78, 79, 80, 99, 112, 116, 117, 119, 120; Oxford City Library: 6, 24, 31, 47, 55, 69, 83; Hertfordshire County Records Office: 8; A. Hosey: 9, 17, 19, 20, 25, 26, 29, 30, 32, 35, 42, 43, 44, 45, 46, 66, 73, 84, 85, 87, 89, 90, 91, 92, 93, 100, 103, 105, 106, 114; Laing Art Gallery & Museum, Newcastle-upon-Tyne: 14, 21, 38, 40, 53, 56, 57, 58, 81, 82, 107, 108, 109, 111, 113; Nottingham Historical Film Unit: 15, 16, 28, 41, 54, 70, 95, 96; Mansell Collection: 18, 59, 60, 72, 94, 118; National Motor Museum: 22, 88; Jack Wilkinson: 27, 34, 75, 86, 97; *Old Motor*: 33, 104; Greater London Council: 39; Devon Library Service (Torquay): 48; Liverpool Public Library: 61, 121; Kodak Museum: 63; Central Library Norwich: 65; John Carter: 68, 77, 115; Victoria & Albert Museum: 71; Birmingham CIty Library Collection: 110.

Introduction

The fair is not a recent phenomenon. Its origins can be traced back to Roman times, the word fair deriving from the Latin for holiday — *feria*. The earliest fairs were for trade — an extension of the market place. Some specialised in the sale of animals; we have horse fairs, sheep fairs, pony fairs and goose fairs, and there was even one at Yarmouth for the herring. Whenever one found a group of people gathered for this type of trade or barter, inevitably there were itinerant traders and with them travelling entertainers such as acrobats, jugglers and fortune tellers.

As fairs became more popular some were legalised and given a charter; records exist of chartered fairs in Norman times. One of the most interesting types of fair is the hiring fair, always held in the autumn. These were large outdoor labour exchanges to which labourers and craftsmen came in search of employment. They paraded through the fair wearing in their lapels or on their caps tokens of their jobs; carters displayed pieces of whip-cord, maids carried mops and these soon became known as mop fairs. A few weeks later another similar fair was often held called the runaway mop, this latter giving those still unemployed a second chance to fix themselves up before the winter. It also gave employers the chance to change any staff that had already proved unsatisfactory.

The travelling fair as we know it today could not come into existence until there were roads good enough to cope with heavy loads. Before the Turnpike Road Acts of 1730 and 1780, the roads of Great Britain were in an appalling condition. For example, it took six horses to draw a small stage coach, and in winter many roads were impassable due to mud. Thomas Telford and John Macadam were the prime movers in road building and surfacing in the 1820s. Until these better roads were made, those travelling from fair to fair usually went on foot or horseback, though wealthier ones might own enough horses to pull a cart. They slept in roadside inns or tents, or slept rough; the caravan did not become popular until roads were improved. With the better highways came greater loads, and the travelling showman with his large sideshows, menageries and elaborate rides was born.

Throughout the nineteenth century the travelling fair developed. First sideshows got bigger, and then came the rides. At first these were hand-driven, but in the latter part of the century steam revolutionised the traditional fairground, being used to power roundabouts and other rides. It was also applied as a prime mover on the road. Electricity then brightened the scene.

In 1874 Thomas Frost wrote this of the travelling fairs: '. . . the railways connect the smaller towns, and most of the villages, with the larger ones in which amusements may be found superior to any ever presented by the old showman. What need then of fairs and shows? The nation has outgrown them, and the last showman will soon be as great a curiosity as the dodo.' Frost had got it wrong, for transport was not as yet readily available — to the working classes at any rate. Tradition dies hard; most of the established town fairs kept going, while the country fair had a place all to itself in the lives of the younger people of the villages. The author can still remember the annual fair and the carnival as being two of the highspots in the life of his native village.

The showmen adapted to the changing ways, presenting only those rides and shows not found in the local town amusement park. As the zoo and the circus became more popular, the travelling menagerie died out. The theatre became established in permanent buildings, so killing off the travelling theatre. Picture palaces became common, so the Bioscope show was relegated to the past. In more recent years the traditional Roundabout lost favour, youngsters preferring the thrills of the Ark or Waltzer or the more modern Jets, Looper or Paratrooper. The Dodgems introduced in the 1920s are still popular, but the cars themselves have to be continually updated to keep in fashion.

Yesterday's rides have not entirely disappeared; there are still a few sets of Galloping Horses (some steam-driven) and Cakewalks. There is even a set of Steam Yachts, too. Although these rides attend a few of the major fairs, most of their time is spent at traction engine rallies and other similar events for 'preserved' transport. Many attempts have been made to re-create the atmosphere of the old-time fair as shown in this book following the highly successful event staged at Shottesbrooke Park, White Waltham, in August 1964, but at the time of writing that pioneer classic has never been surpassed.

This book attempts to depict the fairground from the mid 1860s, a time when a few enterprising photographers turned their cameras onto the social scene, up to the outbreak of World War II. During this period we saw the heyday of the fairground; steam came in to transform the rides, but then declined with the rise of the diesel lorry and generator: inevitably, some of the glamour was lost.

1 One of the origins of the fair as we know it today was the traditional horse fair. A few years ago it looked as if they were likely to disappear but quite a number of these events have survived up and down the country and are enjoying a new lease of life. Perhaps the largest of all the horse fairs is the one staged on the outskirts of Appleby, Cumbria, during June. This is attended by dealers from a very wide area. Another important one is Lee Gap Fair at West Ardsley, outside Wakefield. This is held on St Bartholomew's Day (24 August) and is followed three weeks and three days later by a similar one-day horse fair. At one time Lee Gap Fair lasted for the whole period, but now only the first and last days are observed, so the fairs are known as 'First Lee' and 'Latter Lee'. The fair shown in this photograph was being held at Alfreton around the turn of the century.

2 The earliest fairs were in the
market place, and many have
traditionally retained the same sites.
Sites such as this present problems
to showmen, as on many occasions
they cannot take up their positions
until after the market has closed and
the stalls have been cleared away, at
say six o'clock in the evening. The
fair has then to be assembled rapidly
in order to open the following day.
However, at South Shields in 1899
the fair has come to the market
place, leaving the market traders to
carry on their regular business
around the fringes.

3 Sir Benjamin Stone photographed these three labourers at
Stratford-upon-Avon Mop Fair in
1899. All are wearing tokens of their
trade indicating that they are looking
for employment.

4 and **5** Two photographs of labourers seeking employment, taken as late as autumn 1912 at the hiring fair at High Wycombe.

4

5

The Tober

6

6 The appearance of the tober or fairground has changed a great deal over the years. This is St Giles Fair, Oxford, in 1868. The showmens' living wagons line St Giles on the left with the stalls facing the pavement, while on the right of the street are the shows and the menageries. St Giles Fair has no charter; it grew out of a much smaller event, the annual Wake of Walton Parish. It is still held every year, on the same site and in nearby Magdalen Street, on the Monday and Tuesday following the first Sunday in September. Until a few years ago the showmen were not allowed to draw onto the site (it is one of the few surviving 'street fairs') before Sunday evening, so the hectic build-up can be imagined. It is acknowledged as being the best two-day fair in the country, and attracts amusements all the way from the eastern counties.

7 To Londoners the annual fairs on Hampstead Heath have always been places to visit. The skyline of the fair has changed a lot since the previous photograph. With the coming of steam, both as power for the shows and for haulage, equipment tended to be bigger and more complicated; the bulky looking Helter Skelter could be easily transported from ground to ground. The tober is decorated with flags and bunting, and market traders selling fruit and vegetables mix with the more traditional fairground attractions on Good Friday 1912. Three separate sites are used for the amusements at 'Happy Hampstead' during holiday times and the public turn up in their hundreds. Everyone in the London area associates Hampstead with fairs at holiday times, but there are others. For those living south of the Thames, those on Blackheath Common are probably the best known.

8 Country fairs have their own particular fascination. Before the coming of public transport in the form of motor buses, and when only the rich could afford a motor car, villagers used to rely heavily for diversion on the local show and fair when it visited their area. The fair was their summer entertainment and in winter there were sometimes concerts, films and magic lantern shows in the local Village Hall. This scene is Harpenden September Fair in 1890. No steam here for power — everything is horse-drawn and there are no big rides. The fair is centred around two large sets of Swings, with supporting side-stuff.

9

10

11

9 The village green or local meadow was the ideal setting for the village fair. This is the annual fair at Pickmere, Cheshire in the 1920s. The centrepiece is the Roundabout, while on the left are the Swings, now renamed Airships. The engine providing the power is Silcock's Burrell No 1675, *The Wonder*. An extension has been fitted to its chimney to carry the smoke away, up and over the fair. The barrel in front of the engine provides refills of water for the boiler.

10 Newcastle-upon-Tyne's fair takes place during the third week of June; it is often called the Temperance Festival. This mammoth fair — one of the largest in the country — attracts showmen from as far afield as London and even Scotland. It is held on Town Moor, only about a mile from the city centre at the side of the Great North Road. Many thousands visit this fair during its eight-day opening, but the climax comes on the closing Saturday when the horse races — the 'Pitman's Derby' — take place just across the road. Newcastle must have the largest fairground of any, as there are nearly thirty acres of land devoted to it. This is the scene of the Newcastle Hoppings at Greenwater Pool in 1914. The Helter Skelter still dominates the sky, while closer to the ground are the Joy Wheel, Gallopers and a Scenic Railway. A set of Steam Yachts is also doing good business. The edge of the fair is full of side-stuff, stalls with only the frontage open to the public. Behind the fair are the many caravans in which the showmen live and travel.

11 Tradition plays a large part in the showman's life. Many of the long established fairs had an official opening, usually with the mayor making a speech from the steps of a large ride and then touring the amusements. Mitcham Fair goes back to the 1700s; here in August 1911 the local dignitaries are seen opening the fair with a huge golden key, $4\frac{1}{2}$ft long, which is referred to as the chartered key of Mitcham, even though this one is not in fact a charter fair. The key is still in use today.

12 The Stratford-upon-Avon Mop was originally a hiring fair and still takes place on 12 October. It opens with a civic procession and there has always been a tradition of ox-roasting, a feature of many of the back-end run (autumn) fairs. This photograph was taken by Sir Benjamin Stone at Stratford in 1895. Behind the ox-roast is Tom Clarke's Switchback and Burrell showman's engine No 1820 *Victoria*, new in 1895. The ox-roast is still part of the Stratford Mop Fairs.

13 Street fairs are the result of long traditions. The annual street fair in Pinner for example goes back to 1336, when it was granted a charter. Here in 1936 the fair is back in town with a set of Gallopers dominating the foreground, sandwiched between a telephone box and the sign of the Red Lion pub. The traffic jams resulting from these street fairs can be imagined. In recent years the police have tended to seal off the street fairs and divert the traffic around them.

14 Many favourite fairgrounds are situated on low lying meadows, near rivers or streams. Before radio became commonplace, there were no weather forecasts for showmen to tune in to and so they had to rely on their own weather knowledge. Such riverside locations were prone to flooding and a sudden cloudburst could bring catastrophe. This photograph is of James Cole's Gondolas caught in the floods at Maidenhead in 1926. The showman has started to dismantle the ride, but has been caught by the rising waters. One of the rides to suffer most from such conditions was the Gallopers; if the owners did not have time to dismantle the platforms, the water would float them upwards, so breaking the legs off the horses.

12

13

14

15 Perhaps the most exciting time to view a fair is after dark. The whole event becomes a glittering array of lights, as is shown here at the Nottingham Goose Fair in 1909. Illumination is provided by dozens of arc lights and naptha flares, and steam and smoke from the engines add to the effect. On the left is Collins's Motor Car Steam Switchback Looping the Loop; a few years before, this ride might have been called the Gordon Bennett Racers or some other topical title, demonstrating how the showmen tried to update their equipment by a change of name.

The Rides

16 The Roundabout in one form or another is the background to the traditional British fair. Crude versions had been in existence on the continent since the middle ages. One of the first to be travelled in this country was Twigdon's riding Machine built in 1855. Here a circular platform was suspended by rods from a centre pole with a series of horses mounted on the platform. Possibly conceived in the first instance for children, it obviously suited adults as well. Motive power was supplied either by a man in the centre pushing it around, or by small boys who were paid to push. Their reward often came in the form of free rides. This photograph is thought to have been taken around 1860, and is probably the earliest photograph in this book.

17 One of the earliest forms of
mechanically propelled Roundabouts
was built by Savages of King's Lynn
in 1880 and operated by the
showman Pat Collins in the
Midlands. This early set, shown at
King's Lynn Mart about 1890, is
driven from underneath by means of
a wheel under each horse; as the
floor of the ride revolves, so these
wheels impart the rocking and riding
motion to the horses. The motive
power was a steam centre-engine
which can be seen on the left of the
trumpet organ. This type became
known as a Platform Ride, as
opposed to the later machines which
had the horses suspended from a
revolving top, the up-and-down
movement to simulate a riding
motion being imparted by means of
cranked rods. Some Roundabouts
which did not have a galloping
motion were called Stills. In this case
the top of the ride has none of the
normal carved rounding boards, but
the centre dome is ornately carved
and painted. Note the tilt rolled back
especially for the photograph to give
more light on the organ. This ride
was known as the 'Boston Riding
School'.

18 A form of ride which has lasted longest on fairgrounds is the Gallopers—a derivation of galloping horses. The simplest name for the Gallopers is of course the Roundabout. In America it is known as the Carousel, but in Britain it has been given many other names such as the Merry-Go-Round, Flying Horses, Joy Ride, Hobby Horse, Carry-Us-All, Whirligig and even Steam Riding Galleries. Roundabouts had been in existence many years before 1832, but in that year a new method for turning them was introduced, both in France and in this country. A man stood at the centre and cranked a handle, the machine being made to spin by a set of gears attached to a worm on the centre shaft. This steam-driven set, photographed around the turn of the century, was owned by R. Edwards whose family is still in the business, operating out of Swindon. It is still in existence but is not travelled at present.

19 Bartletts was a firm of showmen who travelled the southern part of England, and one of their rides was this set of three-abreast Gallopers, seen sometime before World War I. The term 'abreast' refers to the number of rows of horses on the machine. The most common type travelled was the three-abreast; the four-abreast was usually restricted to more permanent sites due to its extra weight. A set of Gallopers could have a fair turn of speed and, to counter the centrifugal force, the rods on which the horses were hung were extended to pass through the loading platform. A grooved slot in the platform allowed the horses to swing out to a certain amount; this enabled the rider to keep his seat in safety. In this case some of the horses have been removed, and a hanging chair substituted. This set travelled until after World War II; when discarded it finished its working days as a stage for jazz concerts. The early traction engine in the background is an adaptation for showman's use of an ordinary steam tractor, with short cab and railway-locomotive type spectacle windows. It is *Majestic*, a Burrell built in 1909.

20

21

22

20 On some sets of Gallopers the horses were exchanged for cockerels, as can be seen on this equipment owned by W. Noble, who travelled extensively in the south of England. The cloth covering the roof of the ride is known as a tilt, and in high winds this had to be rolled back to prevent damage to the ride. The centre pole which extends above the tilt was also the chimney of the steam engine in the centre. The organ in the middle was used to draw the crowds to the ride. Most machines of this sort carried flags over the top rounding boards as decoration. A horse normally carried one passenger whereas, as will be seen from this view, the cockerels were double-seaters. On some rides, however, horses were also double-seaters. This photograph was taken in the Isle of Wight around 1919 or 1920 when the Gallopers were travelling with Arnold Brothers'

Bioscope Show. The Bioscope Show was doing very well and taking money, but the Gallopers were not so successful. The owner had to borrow money to pay the boat fare to bring them over to the Island; because of the bad season, he even had to borrow more to return them to the mainland.

21 Another very early type of riding machine was the Sea-on-Land, first produced by Savage in conjunction with the famous circus proprietor 'Lord' George Sanger. Some twenty sets of these were built between 1880 and 1885. They travelled for many years, this one being seen at a Newcastle-upon-Tyne fair in June, 1914. The patrons would ride in the mock yachts; a patented gearing underneath would impart a rocking and pitching motion. The ride is steam driven and is fronted by a trumpet barrel organ.

22 Some children were perhaps a little worried about climbing onto the horses on a full-scale set of Gallopers, so a simpler form of ride was developed for them. The horses were hung much closer to the ground, which made mounting much easier. In early days, a Pony Roundabout such as this would have been turned by a pony walking around the centre column, rotating it as he went. The RSPCA thought this was cruel, and such practices were stopped. Steam power was often substituted, as in this case on Hampstead Heath in the early 1900s.

23

23 Here in close-up we see a Juvenile Roundabout or Dobby Horse riding well on Hampstead Heath in 1912. This is a hand-cranked set; the man on the left is turning the handle.

24 A version of the popular Gallopers was the Flying Pigs. Here we see pigs instead of horses, or other animals and balloons. The balloons were an innovation in that they were allowed to revolve on their own axes as the ride went round. Later this type of ride evolved into the Waltzer. This photograph was taken at St Giles Fair in Oxford in 1908 when the price for a ride was only a penny. Showmen were quick to adapt new ideas to the fairground; though ballooning had been popular for some years, it was not much publicised until the early 1900s. Soon after the balloon had appeared on the fairground it was replaced by the aeroplane in one form or another.

25 In the 1880s, Savages of King's Lynn developed a new type of ride based on the Galloper centre. This was the Switchback, which later became known as the Ark, Speedway, Autodrome, Scenic Railway or Caterpillar. Here the horses are replaced by cars or motorcycles moving on an undulating track. This one was a juvenile version travelled by S. Smart; again it is worked by a steam centre-engine, with the organ facing the crowds. An outer platform allowed spectators to watch the ride and gave easy access to the cars when stationary. This particular photograph was used by the

showman as an advertising card in the 1920s, hence the words 'Fetes and flower shows attended on shortest notice'. Until relatively modern times, a number of travellers possessing one ride and a few items of side-stuff would often journey from place to place without much advance booking. If they found a suitable paddock, orchard or village green, they would pull in and build up the fair. Hence they could easily alter their journeys to take in shows 'on shortest notice'. In many of these photographs it is easy to single out the owner of the ride; he is always the man with the waistcoat and the watch-chain.

26 Farrar's Scenic Whales was fitted with a very large 112-key Gaudin Organ. The organ with its show front takes up the entire width of the centre of the ride. The size of the organ and the carved whales on the cars can be judged by comparison with the size of the figures in the foreground. This set of whales was later destroyed by fire. Part of the very finely painted top rounding boards can be seen above the pillars. This photograph was possibly taken just after World War I.

27 The Chairoplane is another ride to be based on a revolving centre. Here the platform remains stationary and the riders are carried in chairs suspended by chains from the revolving top. In full flight, a set of chairs is an exciting ride to see, with the riders swinging far out over the watching public. This German-built set is seen at Drypool Green Fair, Hull, in 1925. The rounding boards are lettered 'American Swing Swing', and it seats a total of thirty-six patrons. Several of these electrically driven rides came over from Germany in 1923, proving popular with the patrons and riding masters alike. The latter approved of them because they required few workmen and only one engine. This ride had been brought to Drypool Green from Girlington on the outskirts of Bradford by a 1905 Fowler Engine, No 10318 *Sunny Boy No 2*. This journey had been accomplished in record time thanks to the solid rubber tyres just fitted to the engine. These became compulsory by law in 1926. The van on the right-hand side is a particularly fine example of a small showman's living van, being only twelve feet in length.

28 The first Cakewalk to visit Nottingham Goose Fair was this example in 1909 belonging to A. Richards of Hull; it had come directly from Fun City at Olympia, London. This was a ride consisting of a number of oscillating platforms on which the patrons were challenged to stay upright as they walked through it. Its name is derived from a Negro dance. Some showmen paid dancers to ride it for hours on end to attract other customers. On the left is an adaptation of the Foden steam wagon, Number 7141, for showmen's use. The wagon has the traditional twisted brass and a dynamo mounted on the front end of the boiler which provides the power for the ride. The larger-than-usual crowd around the Cakewalk is due to the presence of the Mayoral party which had just opened the 1909 fair, and were having a ride on the machine. Behind and to the left, can be seen the front of Bostock & Wombwell's Menagerie.

29

30

29 Nowadays visitors to a traction engine rally or similar event are quite accustomed to seeing many different types of fairground organ in preservation. Usually they are presented by their owners from the backs of motor lorries or trailers, as this is the easiest way for them to be transported. In the heyday of the fair, these great mechanical instruments featured at the front of the shows or in the centre of the rides. The idea, quite simply, was to attract the flattie (fairground patron) to the show. Showmen vied with each other to have the most highly decorated organ, or preferably the loudest! They were often badly out of tune, very much in the way that records amplified over the average fairground speaker to day are almost unrecognisable. On smaller fairs however, there were often no big rides, so the showman might have just one big organ strategically placed to attract visitors to the fair itself. One such was used by Arnold Brothers in the south of England, seen here in 1931. In the 1930s when there was widespread trade depression, a lot of showmen replaced organs with a loud-speaker system or panatrope so as to keep in business. The big organs were operated by using books of cardboard 'music'; they needed a permanent attendant, and it also meant another load on the road. So the panatropes, which were worked from a turntable in the roundabout's paybox and used cheap gramophone records, saved a man's wage and an extra load.

30 It is unusual to find a period photograph of an organ away from its ride or show. Here we see the large Military Band Organ owned by the West Country firm of Anderton and Rowland at the works of Orton and Spooner where its show front was designed and fitted in 1906. This 98-key Marenghi organ was first of all fitted into a Bioscope Show. Later, when such shows went out of fashion, it was cut down and put into a scenic ride. The organ is still owned by the De Vey family (née Anderton) and is regularly shown at traction engine rallies.

31 One of the tallest rides at any fair is the Big Wheel, sometimes known as the Eli Wheel or Ferris Wheel. Versions of this have been known for many years, but with the coming of steam bigger and better wheels could be produced, as well as ones which revolved faster. This picture was taken at an Oxford Fair in 1895 and clearly shows the stationary steam engine which was used to drive the wheel.

32

33

32 The Dodgem track was first patented in 1921, but it had been preceded by the Brooklands Speedway, an oval track around which the cars raced. Usually the cars were electrically driven but in this case small petrol engines are used. In practice these were not as reliable as the electric variety. This set is by Supercar of Leamington Spa, and was photographed at King's Lynn in 1939. The fairground organ for drawing crowds to the ride has been superseded by the panatrope, a loudspeaker mounted on the top of the central paybox and playing popular music from records.

33 The most common version of the Dodgem or Bumper Car was this type, powered by electricity collected from the overhead wire mesh. Dodgem tracks were usually fully covered and brightly lit. This picture was taken at the May Day Fair at Knutsford Heath in 1936. The Dodgems is a ride which has stood the test of time, and is still a firm favourite. In the early days the cars gave a lot of trouble, and it was possible to see more out of action than those in actual use. Large tracks were frowned upon by showmen, as they discovered that cars reached a much higher speed, and damage from bumping was much greater. As with motor cars, body design has altered. When television came into general use, it cost Dodgem owners quite a lot to fit suppressors to their fleets. If house holders suffered ruined picture reception they would take steps to abolish the fair!

34 One of the new machines to come out of the 1930s was the Moon Rocket. Charles Openshaw of Reading patented the idea in 1936, and it is illustrated here in one of its simplest forms. The thrill of the ride is obtained from the speed at which the cars travel and the centrifugal force created by use of a slope. This is a German-made machine at a Newcastle-upon-Tyne Fair in 1938, owned by the showman John Collins. Many Moon Rockets are far more ornate than this one with elaborate top rounding boards; some had a counter-rotating centre to heighten the effect. Moon Rockets were built in Britain by R. J. Lakin of Streatham.

35 One of the simplest forms of ride was the Swing, a slightly more complicated version of the childrens swings found in parks or playgrounds. In fact this ride was often called a Park Swing. Usually it consisted of a boat carrying two or more people, who pulled on overhead ropes to set it in motion. A later version shown here is known as Over the Tops, Looping the Loop, or Bird Cages. The circular cage always remained horizontal, and the efforts of the caged patrons provided the action. It was every rider's aim to get the cage to go over the top. This is a set owned by Arnold Brothers just before the last war. Note the prominently placed loudspeaker.

36 The Helter Skelter is one of the oldest features of the fairground; sometimes it is called the Lighthouse Slip, now often shortened to purely 'Slip'. It has the advantage of having no mechanical components, the participants sliding down the spiral chute by gravity. Here the Slip dominates South Shields Market Square around the turn of the century. Like the Big Wheel, the Slip is often used as a beacon to attract punters to the fair at night, but this photograph was taken before electricity was widely used for this purpose. At this time, however, the ride would have been illuminated at night with the aid of naptha flare lamps, the traditional lighting of the fairground and the market. One such lamp, for example, would have been hung on the pole which can be seen at the top of the Slip at right angles to it.

The Slip was a difficult amusement to build, and was vulnerable to strong winds, but once erected, it gave trouble-free operation. The proprietor usually sat in a paybox at the top of the lower staircase; the rider was given a mat to sit on and then climbed the stairs and slid down. There was a man at the bottom to assist; he also stacked the mats in a neat pile for future patrons. There are some modern Slips of lattice-work construction, much smaller and better suited to windy conditions.

37 An unusual view of a Helter Skelter taken from the top looking down on two fairgoers descending in tandem. At the bottom a crowd has collected to watch the antics of those finishing the trip. Those in the know slow themselves down before they reach the bottom—otherwise they tend to shoot straight off the finishing pad into the crowd. One modification to the Slip was the Bowl Slide which finished with the patrons circling a bowl at the end of the trip. Much amusement was caused by their efforts to climb out.

38 One of the most exciting rides ever to be presented on the fairground were the Steam Yachts. They were a development of a steam swing produced by Henry Cracknell and William Cartwright in the late 1880s. Savages of King's Lynn built two sets in 1894, and it was their version which became known as the Yachts. The drive came from a portable steam engine in the centre and was connected to the two boats by a chain; the steam engine is behind the organ in the centre under the awning. Baker's Steam Yachts are seen here at a Newcastle fair in June, 1914; on this occasion they were riding at 1d all classes. The boats were named *Lusitania* and *Mauretania.*

39

40

CODONA'S NEWFIGURE8 RAILWAY.

39 A much earlier version of Over the Tops was this Overboat, which was in a way a very small Big Wheel. The highly ornate boats were suspended within a square frame which in turn was operated from a central point. Some were hand cranked, others worked by steam and later by electricity. The patrons would often swing the boat as well. This is a rare set of two—a double set of Overboats. In order to maintain balance (to even out the load) it was frequently necessary to add heavy weights in one of the cars, particularly on hand-operated sets. This pre-World War I scene is in the London area, probably on Hampstead Heath.

40 Some riding masters in the North of England got together in the late 1920s to form the Palm Beach Amusement Company. One of the rides they travelled was a Figure of Eight, a smaller version of the Big Dipper, a ride more usually associated with permanent amusement parks, often at the seaside. The Figure of Eight was only suitable for really big fairs since building up took a considerable time and required extra workmen. In relation to the distance travelled by the patron, this is a very compact and thrilling ride, but operating costs prevented it from enjoying great popularity amongst the showmen. In this view can be seen a truck lettered 'John Murphy's Proud Peacocks'. This is one of the scenery trucks with low arched roofs, which made them suitable for rail transit as they came within the limits of the loading gauge.

41 A ride for the young or those trying to show off to their friends, the Joy Wheel had only limited popularity with the travelling showman. The idea was for the patrons to try and stay on a rapidly revolving disc, which often had a conical centre. This is Collins' Joy Wheel at Nottingham Goose Fair in 1910. The price of admission included the facility to watch or ride as you wished. The Joy Wheel did not last very long, as it was not suited to all members of the family. In the 1920s an attempt was made to revive the Joy Wheel with a 'miniature edition' in the form of the Devil's Disc, but it too was short-lived and very few were built. They were the type of ride the showman called a 'oncer'—as few people would come back for a second try.

42 The Devil's Disc was a spinning ride, enclosed on three sides; the fronts often had incredible painted decor such as this. Here the fairground decorator has really been able to let rip, and the result must have been thought very daring for the period, the 1920s. The fairground workers posing amongst the frolics are completely dwarfed by the monstrous and almost obscene characterisation of life in Hell.

43 As the taste of the general public began to change, showmen modified the style of painting on their rides. This is Farrars' Super Speedway. Gone is the Victorian style of decoration—a much more modern type has taken its place. This ride would not look out of place in a fair today. The paintwork would last many years if it was carefully looked after and would be regularly scrubbed, touched up and varnished. Each item would be separately packed away to avoid scratching and chafing. Note the hundreds of electric light bulbs on this ride.

The Shows

44 In the early years of the century, it was the shows which were the major attractions at fairs. The public rarely ventured far from home in those days and relied on entertainments being brought to them. One very popular crowd puller was what was then called 'The Wild Beasts Show', and there were several of them. Most of the people had their first glimpse of such animals at the travelling menagerie, since permanent zoos were practically unknown. Best known of this kind of show was Bostock & Wombwell's Menagerie which travelled throughout the British Isles, showing on its own, but always attended the October fairs at Nottingham and Hull. A band played on the front as an inducement to patrons. It often showed for one-day stands in the smaller towns and villages. As early as 1840 Wombwell had no less than twenty-nine different animals travelling, including twelve lions, eight tigers, three elephants and three giraffes. This scene is at Hull at the eight-day fair in 1919. The large crowd is typical of the period, and the pelican is also being used as a front-of-the-house attraction.

46 Pat Collins' Bioscope Show was one of the largest travelling. It was decorated by 5,600 coloured lights, and featured in the centre a magnificent 98-key Marenghi Organ. This great organ has been preserved, and is now owned by Bill Hunt of Oldbury. One of the traction engines which supplied the power can be seen on the extreme right. At one time, Pat Collins travelled four big shows, and needed as many as twenty-five traction engines to transport them. Later he opened a chain of permanent cinemas in the Midlands.

45 Moving pictures, as the early films were known, came into being before the turn of the century and showman Randall Williams introduced them to the fairground in 1896, claiming them to be the greatest scientific invention of the age. In view of their immense popularity, many other showmen concentrated on this new form of entertainment, and they were known on the fairs as Bioscope Shows. Permanent cinemas came into being before World War I, and thus ended the days of the Bioscope on the fairgrounds. In the south, however, Arnold Brothers ran their Bioscope Show up until 1922, when it was sold, and in the middle 1920s Bingo Cinema used to appear in a few Scottish villages. The superb frontage of Jacob Studt's Bioscope is typical of many. There is a mechanical organ on one side of the entrance with possibly as many as 110 keys, and a traction engine on the other. It is interesting to see how the carved work has been adapted to fit on to the traction engine's awning, as it stands in front of the show. Such shows were brilliantly illuminated, in this case with twenty-two arc lights. In the centre is a royal coat of arms to show that the Bioscope had been attended by royalty. Behind the frontage was a simple rectangular tent which could accommodate up to 1,000 people in which the films were shown.

47 A fair such as Oxford St Giles would have many different types of show. Here in 1885 two differing ones were built up alongside; on the left is Lawrence's Anglo-American Marionettes, an extraordinary puppet show, while on the right Chittock has performing dogs and monkeys. The marionette show is in progress, and Chittock has started his front-of-the-house show to draw in the next batch of patrons. The crowds are being entertained by a drummer and trumpeter accompanying the barrel organ, plus a few of the performing monkeys. The barker or spieler has yet to make his announcements. Each show vied with the other for custom, so prices had to be competitive. Admission to Chittock's was 3d.

As horses were used for moving the loads from one fairground to another, the rolling stock had to be limited in size and weight. Each show was made up of a number of different wagons: the wheels of some of these can be seen underneath the frontage of Lawrence's marionettes.

48 With the coming of the cinematograph, films were often incorporated in beast shows. A screen could be lowered on rollers in front of a cage of lions for example, the animals keeping up a continuous roar throughout the silent film. Here at Torquay Regatta Fair about 1900 the front-on-the-house show is on at Hancock's Palace, with two children boxing. On the left is the showman's engine while on the right can be seen a large organ. Jones's Circus Varieties on the right was an adaptation of the traditional circus to the fairground sideshow.

49 and **50** Serious theatre was at one time part of the fairground scene, when bands of travelling actors would set up amongst the other sideshows. If the people were unable to get to the theatre, then the theatre came to the people. They used the same attractions on the front as other shows, the organ for example, as well as actors who played a small part of the show free to the waiting crowds. This is Holloway's show at Birmingham, June 1903. One wonders how many of the old music halls, variety theatres and cinemas took their names from the shows on the fairgrounds.

51 and **52**   Before television provided mass entertainment, there were numerous theatres showing variety. Many people preferred a 'live' show to pictures. When the variety show opened, there was usually some spectacular dancing by the chorus girls, and the 'high steppers' added a touch of glamour. On the fairgrounds the paraders danced on the show front to tunes played on the organ, and they certainly attracted the crowds. The outside show was entirely free. *Top*, the can-can girls performing out front at Stratford-upon-Avon Mop Fair in 1908. *Below*, the more modern equivalent at Mitcham Fair limbering up behind the scenes before appearing out front.

53 The coming of the Cinematograph and the Bioscope Shows rendered the more traditional theatre shows obsolete. Mammy Paine's Coliseum changed from theatre to acts of mystery and conjuring. At the same time, they announced on large notices outside that theirs was not a picture show, it was real live entertainment. It is interesting to see that here, in the early 1920s, at Newcastle-upon-Tyne, virtually every member of the crowd is wearing a hat!

54 Front-of-the-house attractions were not confined to dancing girls. The menagerie shows used to display some of their animals. In the case of Bostock & Wombwell's Menagerie, Billy the pelican was a favourite for many years. Here he is seen at a Nottingham Goose Fair, probably after World War I. Wearing all the medals is the star of the show—Captain Fred Wombwell—who must surely be the most famous wild animal trainer of all time. To see him enter the lions' cage and put the animals through their paces was an unforgettable sight. While the lions growled and snarled, Captain Wombwell would shout orders in a voice like thunder. Backstage, however, the Captain was very quietly spoken, and a more affectionate couple than he and his wife would be difficult to find. But performing with wild animals in such a restricted space as a 'beast van' called for great agility; rheumatism forced the Captain to relinquish his position as ace performer during the menagerie's last few years on the road. It was then when Captain Wombwell set up a stall in the menagerie where, for a few copper coins, the youngsters could buy apples, buns, etc, for feeding the animals. No scales were used—it was a 'handful' a time, so the wise ones always bought from the Captain, as he had the biggest hand! The placards on the front of the show read 'Grander and better than ever for this visit', 'See the Wilde Beaste or horned horse', 'See the baby tigers, the first ever born with a travelling menagerie', 'See the almost human apes'.

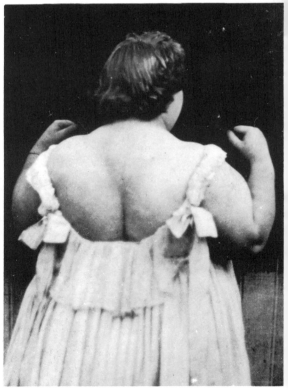

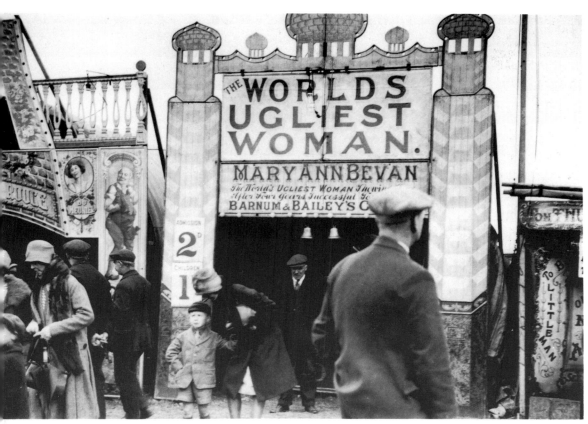

55 Many years ago sports were part of the fair, particularly in country areas. As the fairs grew up, boxing and wrestling became part of the established travelling scene. Even in the television age, the few remaining boxing and wrestling booths are still popular and some wellknown champions have come from the booths. It was a tough life on the booths; on one occasion at the Durham Miners' Gala of 1919, Billy Wood of Dumfries fought eighteen fights in one day, stopping fifteen of his opponents within the distance, and the miners could be very tough. Some would travel to five different fairs in eight days, fighting some eight times a day, as well as pulling down the booth, travelling to the next venue and building up again. This is Oxford St Giles Fair in 1898 and it is interesting to see that the proprietor is trying to attract the ladies as well as the gentlemen.

56 and **57** Freak Shows have always been a popular line with showmen. Some were live shows, others used stuffed animals. All manner of animal freaks have been shown, but it is the human element which really attracts the customers. Nowadays they are mainly dwarfs, giants, very thin or very fat people. There are a few tattooed ladies, but people are too sensitive to pay money to see people with deformities. Beautiful Marie was a fat lady, but as here in the 1900s she was young, she was billed as a giant schoolgirl. Outside the booth the showman uses a trumpet barrel organ to draw in the crowds while inside Marie does not seem to be quite as fat as the artist's drawing. Shows presenting animal freaks are under fire these days, as there are frequent objections by 'animal lovers'.

58 Mary Ann Bevan had a sad life; she left home at an early age and went to work on a Kent farm. She married and had four children, and her husband was killed in World War I. She developed an incurable disease which affected her facial characteristics, as well as enlarging her hands and feet. One day she read about a competition with a £100 prize to find the ugliest woman in the world; she entered and won. She later travelled widely with the fairs and died at the age of 45. On the Mary Ann Bevan show can be seen two brass bells. These were popular with those presenting shows, and much more effective than the loud hailers of today.

59 The coming of the microphone and loudspeaker made the spieler's job much easier, as can be seen at Norwich Fair in 1937. The half man, half woman was a common form of sideshow at one time; with careful training it was possible for a person to develop muscles and other characteristics on one side of the body only. This one is competing with a girlie show. Oriental mysteries are now a thing of the past, since they are not daring enough for the modern fairgoer; strip shows have taken their place. Long established showmen have a very high sense of morality; to them the strip show is anathema.

60 Fortune tellers have been part of the fairground scene from the earliest days. Nowadays they operate out of expensive caravans, but for many years they used small tents which they carried around with them, often on foot. Phillip Allingham in his book *Cheapjack* describes his first fortune telling booth: 'I was getting short of cash, but I bought a garden shelter at Gamage's for thirty-five shillings. I also purchased an incense-holder, some incense, and a number of eastern trays from Woolworths, and when I had draped some cloth across the open front of my shelter it made a pretty good fortune telling booth.' There could be as many as one hundred fortune tellers at a big fair such as Hull. The small tents used by what were known as 'tick offs' had one big disadvantage to the palmist: when the fair was closed they were the obvious choice for a toilet.

61 Thomas Burke took this photograph of a Liverpool fair in 1895. Throwing games have always been one of the most popular sideshows, often called Aunt Sally Shows. 'Three balls a penny' used to be the charge. By the expression on this lady's face, trade must have been very bad indeed though it must be admitted that there is very little to attract the public to this stall.

62 One tends to think of the Coconut Shy as a sideshow of long standing. However during the 1800s coconuts were an expensive fruit and the earliest form of this game was for the punter to hurl large sticks at baskets balance on poles at the back of the booth. Many of the stalls retain the red sheets with white lettering of the type seen before World War I. Here trade looks busy on the Coconut Shy at Hampstead Heath in June 1922.

63 Games involving shooting at targets with rifles have always had a high popularity, even where showmen give no prizes to the successful. This is a small and neat travelling shooting gallery, seen on Hampstead Heath in 1898, where the customers are trying to shoot the bowls off clay pipes. This particular show is mounted on a hand barrow to keep weight down. There is very little protection behind the stall to catch stray shots, and no sides to contain ricochets. Stalls such as this would not be tolerated at a modern fair because of the lack of safety precautions.

64 and **65**　Though there is only one Wall of Death currently travelling in this country, it still pulls in packed houses wherever it goes. Traditionally the building is shaped like a farm silo with the riders performing on the inside and the public viewing the show from a gallery at the top. The most usual form of Wall features motorcycle riders giving exhibitions of all sorts of trick riding on the vertical sides of the wooden drome. Tommy Messham nowadays includes a

bicycle rider as a contrast! The idea of using midget cars came from the United States in the 1920s, and in order to give greater thrills lions as sidecar passengers were quite extensively used. Barry's Sensational Motordrome *(top)* pictured at a Norwich Fair in 1939 was one of the last to use this trick. The driver carrying a lion as passenger *(below)* is the American lion tamer Mr Egbert who was performing at a Mitcham fair in the 1930s.

66 A simpler version of the Wall of Death was the Globe of Death. Here in 1922 the riders performed inside a globe with slatted sides which allowed the visitors to view it from outside, so eliminating a great deal of structure to be carried about and erected. An even simpler version of the Globe has appeared as an act in theatres; this was known as the Saucer, since only the top part of the globe was used. As a finale the Saucer would be lifted to the top of the stage with a rider circling in it. The motorcycles used in these shows were usually highly modified versions of large-capacity American machines such as Indians or Harley Davidsons. Often the frame would be shortened, the forks reinforced and extra leaves added to the springs. The handlebars would be altered, and all road equipment removed. The riders were responsible for the preparation of their own machines; any mechanical fault which developed when they were travelling at up to 45mph could have been fatal.

67 Showmen play heavily on the ego. Get a crowd around a Striker and he can drum up any number of customers to have a go. In theory, the harder you hit the base of the Striker the further the market goes up the pole, and if you are lucky it will ring the bell. No prizes here, you do it just for the honour and glory. Get a group of young men and their girls, and their desire to show off will keep the money rolling in. This is Hampstead Heath in 1930, with two girls obviously posing for the press photographer. A few Strikers have survived. At one time there were juvenile Strikers and the child always got a prize of some sort, determined by where the indicator stopped.

68 Arcades of slot machines are very numerous at fairs today, but they were late arrivals on the fairgrounds. One of the first to introduce them was Birmingham showman Joe Fletcher, in the early 1920s. They were not too popular with showmen as many local by-laws forbade 'games of chance', and the police were very active in stopping their appearance in such areas. Many types of slot machines were to be found; the seaside 'What the Butler Saw' or the ones which told your fortune were the most common. Others produced an X-ray picture of the patron or even a picture of his mother-in-law! There were many ball games, such as this football one, where you paid 2d and the winner received 1d back.

Popular with the teenagers was the Punchball Machine and 'Test Your Grips' which showed on a clock dial the number of pounds you could grip. A version of the latter had an electric coil and dry battery, and by gripping and turning the handle, you could increase the electric shock given; a dial showing you the amount of shock you could take.

69 Showmen have a tradition of being a God-fearing race. Many of the mighty organs had a large repertoire of hymn tunes and other religious music. The Oxford Bible Stall is an example of a religious group taking their beliefs to the people at Oxford St Giles Fair in 1880. Around this time, however, there would normally be no fairs or Bioscope Shows on Sundays. The late Mrs Arnold is reputed to have told the story that when, for the first time, Arnold Brothers opened their Bioscope Show on a Sunday (in Somerset in 1908), disaster struck soon afterwards. There was a very bad storm that evening which blew down half the show. It was regarded by locals and fairground folk as retribution for opening on the Lord's Day. In later years when Sunday opening became more commonplace, there was often a religious service conducted from the steps of the Gallopers before the fair opened. Religious groups are still to be seen at the really big fairs, such as Newcastle, Hull and Nottingham.

70 A traditional part of the fair from the middle ages onwards was the hawker who, with very little equipment, attended the gatherings selling whatever he could lay his hands on. The coming of compulsory licences for such traders has reduced their numbers drastically. In 1911 this hawker in Nottingham is selling tickling sticks, monkeys on a stick, bags of confetti, balls on a piece of elastic, and many strings of beads. Also on sale would have been 'ladies' tormentors', a lead tube around 3½in long filled with water. The water would be squirted onto girls attending the fair and then the poor unfortunate lady would be showered with confetti. Sometimes showmen would apparently take pity on girls who had been covered in confetti and offer to turn them upside down and shake the confetti out of their clothes. They would then collect together the fallen confetti and re-sell it! After the fair closed, they would also collect up the discarded tubes and refill them with water for sale the next day.

71 and **72** Ever since the first fairs, people have been peddling food at these gatherings. Here, at the turn of the century, we see a lemonade stall and also one selling whelks and jellied eels. Another very popular stall was the panam, which sold such items as coconuts, brandy snaps and other sweetmeats. Items such as tea and sandwiches were unobtainable in the early days. At modern fairs, of course, you will find many stalls tempting you to buy hot dogs, hamburgers, fish and chips or candyfloss.

Building Up
& Pulling Down

73 To the layman, building up a fair must appear as a chaotic process. To the showman however, it is a very precise operation. The rides must be built up completely level, whatever the slope of the ground may be. Here is a view of King's Lynn market place in 1925 with the annual fair in course of erection. Recognised by showmen as the opening event of the season, King's Lynn Mart (a charter fair still held annually on the centrally located site), commences on 14 February, St Valentine's Day. Farrar Brothers are building up their Scenic Whales, the Switchback track is in position, and the centre truck (containing the organ around which will be built the scenery) has been raised up on blocks. Farrars' Fowler Engine *Reliance* can be seen on the left of the organ, and on the right is Ling's Fowler *The Great Bear.* Both belong to Doncaster-based showmen, evidence of the importance of this fair to amusement caterers. The gigantic whales in which the patrons will ride on the Scenic Railway are sheeted in the foreground. On the right-hand side of the picture is an engine sheeted over, probably one of Thurston's Burrells.

74 Building up at Barnet Fair in 1919. The Helter Skelter on the left is being built up from within, and the chutes around the side will be put on last of all. The Gallopers still have to have their horses fixed to the poles; after this the floor of the ride will be built up. The Scenic and Joy Wheel have apparently been completed. The painting on the Slip is made to resemble the stonework of a lighthouse. Fitting the outside 'chutes' started at the bottom, and sections were carried up them singly until the top was reached. This was not easy, for anyone holding one of those heavy chutes (a two-handed job) was apt to slip, and then slide right down to the bottom.

75

75 On many sites it was difficult for showmen to build up on flat land. Here at Chipping Norton Mop Fair they have been given a very tricky site to work, on a distinct slope. Nowadays this would not be tolerated. When building up, much packing material would be needed under the ride to even it up and it was virtually impossible for a patron to mount the ride on the far side. Ideally, a riding master would wish his patrons to be evenly spread around his machine, so taking the strain off the mechanism. In this situation it is obviously an impossibility unless he is riding full. To stop patrons all climbing on at once, the driver would never quite stop the ride. The showman's engine in the background is an Aveling and Porter; the photograph was taken around 1920.

76 While most of the work of setting up a fair has to be manual, mechanisation has been applied in some instances. Here a Scenic Railway is being built up; the centre and the organ are in position and so is the track. The heaviest item is however, the set of cars in which the patrons ride. These are being lifted onto the track by a crane fixed to the bunker of a scenic showman's engine. These cranes were capable of lifting some 30cwt; the winch on the engine provides the lift. This picture was taken at Barnet Fair in September, 1923. Car-lift cranes were introduced about 1918, as the brainwave of Bradford showman Goldthorpe Marshall. In view of their immediate success they subsequently became standard equipment on all engines of scenic type. The steel wire rope fitted to the engines came in useful for this extra duty.

77 Preparations are in hand for the opening of the fair at Barnet around 1915. The cars on Abbott and Barker's Scenic Railway have been uncovered and the round stall on the right is ready for business. In this instance, the showman's engine was only providing power for the lights which were not required until dusk, so it is still sheeted and the fire unlit. The Scenic Railway has its own centre engine to provide the motion. Note the beautiful pillars on the ride; they would have been skilfully painted to give a marbled effect. The extreme height of these pillars is unusual. The round stall on the right is a version of the Hoopla 'rings and blocks'. The table is covered by a lovely velvet cloth which would have been decorated with gold embroidery and golden tassels.

78 Fairground rides are always highly decorated, with many parts. When a showman has two or even three fairs to cover in a week, he must be sure his loads are packed carefully to avoid damage. Pieces must always be put back into the packing truck in just the right order for getting them out again. Often they are numbered to facilitate this process. Here, at Hampstead Heath in 1932, Harry Gray's Ark is being packed up. There had been a storm deluge the previous day and the ground is like a quagmire. Most packing trucks are fitted with front or side belly boxes under the main platform to provide extra storage space. In horse-drawn days, these were usually at the front or the back, as the large wheels would have precluded the fitting of any at the side. A front belly box is clearly shown in this photograph. The story is told of a fairground worker and his wife who slept for ten years in one of these front belly boxes.

79 It usually takes a full day to build up a large ride, but it can be done more quickly should the need arise, and if there are enough staff. They come down more quickly; often a fair would pull down on a Saturday night, move on to a new ground overnight, build up on Sunday, and open again on Monday. Nottingham Goose Fair, for example, closes just before midnight on the Saturday, and many of the showmen are open again at Hull for 11 o'clock on the Monday morning. Here at Mitcham in 1936 a gaff worker is taking a Juvenile Galloper horse and cockerel to the packing truck. When a fair is being built up, usually the big machines are dealt with first; then the juveniles and side-stuff are built around them. The reverse procedure is adopted when pulling down. Hence in this case the Juvenile is being dismantled, while the Chairoplanes remain built up in the background. The chairs have been tied up to prevent any of the children from trying to swing on them!

80 After the fair is over . . . . Many of the big rides have already been dismantled and moved on, leaving behind a rearguard of workers to clear up the fairground here at Hampstead in the 1930s. In some cases there was not enough transport available to take all the loads in one go, so the living vans were left and the engines returned for them later. It was imperative that the fairground should be left clean and tidy after the fair had moved on, otherwise there was a good chance that the showmen would not be allowed back the following year.

78

Power on the Road
& for the Rides

81 Moving a fair on the road has always been a complicated business. In horse-drawn days of course loads were limited, though it was not unusual to see as many as six horses pulling trucks from some of the larger shows. Because the loads had to be broken down into smaller units there were more of them. There is in existence a photograph of Sedgwick's Menagerie halted between fairs which shows thirteen horse-drawn trucks. This photograph is of Bostock & Wombwell's Menagerie on the move in 1913. The vans used for accommodating wild animals obviously had to be of exceptional strength; they were, therefore, of enormous weight too.

82 The Menageries were at a slight advantage when it came to transport as they could harness one or two of their animals; in this case an elephant is pulling the load at the Newcastle-upon-Tyne in 1913. Certain more docile animals could also be hitched on behind, so saving another wheeled vehicle. At one Nottingham Goose Fair held on the Forest site, heavy rain had turned the Tober into a morass and the traction engines were bogged down when it came to leaving, but a travelling zoo scored by having the elephant to assist in rescue work. Before the advent of the Showman's Guild and better organisation, it was a case of first come first served at any new ground. Hence the dash from one venue to another was often hectic. Lord George Sanger tells of a battle between Hilton and Wombwell's Menagerie on the Reading to Henley Road. The Wombwell drivers tried to overtake the others in their efforts to get to Henley in time to secure the best places. Caravans were overturned, beast wagons broken open and the animals allowed to escape. Sanger writes: 'We had a good day after all for business, though it was the sorriest lot of battered performers and damaged caravans that Henley Fair had ever witnessed.'

84 With a full head of steam, T. Smith and Sons' Foden Showman's Engine No 528 is winched away from Victoria Park Fairground, Hayward's Heath, Sussex, in August 1939, after becoming bogged in the muddy ground. The engine is fitted with rubbers on the wheels; all the caravans have small wheels with pneumatic tyres which made for easier running on the roads and higher overall speeds. The two engines doing the winching are Tasker tractors No 1770 and 1675.

83 With the coming of the steam traction engine, showmen quickly adapted it for their purposes. One of these was to pull the loads from one fairground to another. Gone were the single trucks pulled by horses; in their stead came the long road train, with its engines hauling as many as ten trailers with a total weight of fifty tons or more. In early times the showman adapted his horse-drawn trucks to the new motive power, hence the long loads. Later came legislation restricting the number of trailers, so special packing trucks were evolved to carry heavier individual loads. Here, around 1910, we see Chipperfield's Electric Theatre, one of the large Bioscope Shows, on the road, drawn by Burrell Showman's Engine No 2281, *Queen of the Midlands.* This engine was built in 1900.

85 On this occasion a defect in the steering mechanism on Burrell No 2803 has made Sangers hastily add shafts and a horse to assist with the steering, or was it a well thought out gimmick to attract the photographers from the local paper? The scene was Torquay, about 1922. The peculiar 'hairnet' over the chimney of the engine is a spark arrester; engines not so fitted have been known to set fire to thatched cottages or corn-fields. In recent years one even started a fire in the grass surrounding an army ammunition dump, to the consternation of the authorities.

86 Before the coming of the steam traction engine, fairground loads were all horse-drawn. Then it was often quicker when moving from one fairground to another, some distance away, to take the loads by rail. The coming of the traction engine did not always change this procedure, for provided that all arrangements were made in advance, it would still be quicker than travelling by road, particularly before rubber tyres on the engines became compulsory. What was tedious, however, was the transportation of the vehicles to the railway station, loading them one by

one at the dock, and reversing the procedure at the other end. For example, when Hull Fair began almost immediately after closing day at Nottingham, the LNE and LMS Railways vied with each other in running special trains for fairground tackle.

W. H. Marshall & Sons used to have a fleet of four big traction engines, and their travelling season started with the Spring Fair at Halifax, a fortnight before Easter. Here we see their Fowler No 10318 at Pellon goods yard; the engine is removing a load of the Hey-Day brought by rail from a Lancashire town; surprisingly this photograph was taken as late as 1936. Virtually no fairs travelled by rail after the last war, but some circuses continued the practice into the 1950s. The cost of moving a load by rail was as little as 6d per mile in 1908. Those travellers accompanying the load had to buy an ordinary rail ticket. Therefore the children were sometimes locked into the living van and instructed to 'keep quiet' for the length of the journey, in the hope that they would not be spotted by the railway authorities. One family is known to have travelled from Gloucester to Eastleigh in this way.

87 Not every traveller could afford one of the large showman's engines; indeed in the early days it was not necessary for him to have one as his rides might well lack electric drive. He did, however, want something to replace horses and take his ride from fair to fair. Some showmen therefore bought steam tractors which they adapted to their requirements. In this case, the Smarts had fitted a full-length cab to a Burrell general purpose road locomotive, but neither a dynamo nor twisted brass columns. They had had the canopy decorated with their name, in gold-leaf lettering. This engine is also fitted with two candle-type carriage lamps at the front. As a matter of interest, the chain from the cab upright is attached to the clothes line!

MESSRS. HANCOCK'S TRACTION ENGINE WITH ITS A

MESSRS. G. TWIGDON & SON'S TRACTION ENGINE *en route* HAULING NINE VANS AND OVER FORTY TONS.

...OAD OF TWENTY-EIGHT TONS *en route* AT DARTMOUTH.

JACOB STUDT'S STEAM CIRCUS *en route*.

88 This is a double-page spread from the 1909 catalogue of Charles Burrell and Sons of Thetford. All the vehicles which are being towed by the traction engines were formerly horse-drawn, which emphasises the great change which took place when steam haulage became regular practice. Though the catalogue illustrates a full showman's engine, it is interesting to see that none of the engines in these photographs are equipped with dynamos, as they are only being used for haulage purposes.

89

90

89 and **90**   Savages built two
unusual engines in 1897 and 1898
which were known as traction
centres. Here was an attempt to use
the same engine for haulage as well
as driving the ride—mechanically as
opposed to electrically. The drive
was taken by vertical gearing
through the cab roof to the centre of
the ride. They were not a great
success. One of these engines, No
728 *Enterprise*, was delivered to
George Baker of Southampton to
drive his set of Gallopers. Prior to
this, Baker had taken delivery of
engine No 1934 from Burrells of
Thetford and had it converted in his
own workshop to a traction centre.
Possibly one was to act as a spare
engine in case of breakdown. It is
unlikely that the dynamo could be
used at the same time as the vertical
drive. This highly ornate decoration
was typical of the period and very
appropriate on the traction centre as
it would have formed part of the
ride's centre decoration. Here we see
the Burrell as built in 1896 and
about 1910-11, some time after
conversion.

91   The steam centre-engine was for
many years the main motive power
for various versions of the
Roundabout. Another adaptation of
it, however, was to drive the Steam
Yacht. Most Steam Yachts were
twin-boat sets and had to be worked
separately from the one boiler, so the
boiler had to operate the engines on
top of it. Each boat could accommodate 20-30 people; to start the
boat it had to be rocked, gently at
first, and gradually more and more.
To do this the engine was run first
one way and then reversed until
sufficient momentum was gained to
make it work automatically there-
after. This is Savage's Steam Yacht
Centre Engine No 883, new in 1921.

Fowler Class R Showmans Scenic type Engine with exciter. No. 15658

92 This is an illustration from a catalogue of John Fowler and Co of Leeds, showing one of their famous showman's scenic engines. 'Scenic' refers to the type of ride that such engine would accompany. Such rides have rise and fall platforms and an extra load is placed on the engine's dynamo when starting the ride with the cars on one of the uphill sections. An ordinary dynamo would throw its driving belt if suddenly subjected to this type of load, so Fowler inserted an exciter on the field side of the dynamo, to boost the power when starting. As this exciter was mounted on top of the boiler, the whole of the engine had to be lengthened.

93 Wallis and Steevens of Basingstoke made only a few showmen's engines, but in 1903 they built this 8 NHP engine for Henry Jennings of Devizes. Jennings gave it the name *Royal John.* It was fitted with a Dickinson dynamo, a make popular with showmen in the earlier days of steam. The extension chimney is in position to carry the smoke away high above the fair. The ornate paintwork is unusual on an engine.

94 A traction engine requires daily maintenance. Many parts require oiling, and the firebox needs cleaning out before the new fire is lit. There are the brasses to be cleaned and the other metal work to be kept shiny. To the riding master, his engine was part of the show, and if he was proud of his ride, he was also proud of his engine and kept it spotlessly clean. After every hundred hours of running, the boiler had to be washed out to remove rust and silt. This was often done on a Sunday when the fair was not on the move. This Burrell belonged to the St Austell-based firm of J. Rowland and is believed to be No 3660 *Victor,* built in 1915 and scrapped in 1950, seen here in the 1930s.

95 The showman's engines which
provided the power were often
situated within the fair itself so that
the drivers could see the person in
charge of the machine, and thus
know when maximum load was
required. This also allowed much
shorter lengths of electric cable to be
used without the resulting loss of
current. Behind the engine is Pat
Collins' Channel Tunnel Railway.
This took the form of a real steam
engine pulling up to six trucks
around a circular track, at least half
of which was in darkness. At the
time of its inception in the late 1880s
it was a great novelty, as many
people had never travelled on a
railway train. Because of the
darkness, it was also much
appreciated by young couples who
made up a high percentage of the
customers. This scene shows the
Goose Fair at the Nottingham
Market Place in 1895, with the Old
Exchange in the background.

96 At each fairground, the showmen had to make sure there was an adequate supply of coal and water for the steam engines. Water was usually stored in barrels nearby or brought in by dandy or water cart. In this scene a lorry is bringing in a new supply of coal for the showman's engine before the fair gets under way; the dragons on Pat Collins' Scenic are still sheeted. While the traction engines usually burnt steam coal, the centre engines on the machines were often coke fired to reduce the risk of sparks falling from the chimney onto the canvas tilts or covers. On the right is Holland's very elaborate Scenic Whales. The engine is Fowler Number 14424 *Dreadnought* which was built to the order of the War Office during World War I and is now preserved under the name of *Goliath*. As the engine is partly standing on the pavement, the driver has levelled it with blocks to keep the boiler 'head-up'. This helps to keep the maximum amount of water back against and around the firebox.

This scene is taken from nearly the same spot as the previous picture, but from a lower vantage point and over thirty years later. It shows the Goose Fair at Nottingham in 1927, the last to be held in the Market Place before being transferred to its present site on The Forest. In the background is the steel framework for the Council House which was then being built to replace the Old Exchange.

97

97 Fun Fairs are popular
attractions for galas and carnivals, so
when Barnsley held a 'Joy Week' in
Locke Park there was quite a big
fair. Unfortunately, however, it took
place in the wettest week of 1936,
despite being held in July. The
grassland site quickly became a sea
of mud. When they came to depart,
the stallholders hired a contractor's
traction engine to extricate their
living vans from the water-logged
ground, paying ten shillings a time.
In a very short time, however, even
this engine sank deeply into the
ground and it took considerable time
to extricate it. This view shows
Harry Hall's big Burrell *The Whale*,
with chains on its driving wheels to
give added grip on the soft ground.
Before the days of rubber tyres, it
was possible for showmen to bolt
pieces of angle iron called 'spuds'
direct to the metal wheels; these
gave superior adhesion under such
adverse conditions. It can be seen
that the driving pins in the rear
wheel have been pulled out, enabling
the engine's winch to revolve freely
so that the wire rope can be used to
pull out the bogged vehicles.

In the background is a Tilling-
Stevens petrol-electric truck, a great
favourite with showmen. A petrol
engine drove a dynamo; this
powered an electric motor, which
provided the final drive. Many
showmen used these lorries much in
the same way as a showman's engine.
After the lorry had pulled the loads
to the ground, the dynamo was used
to provide lighting for the show.

98 Many showmen took advantage
of the large number of ex-War
Department lorries which came on
the market after World War I. Most
of these were fully reconditioned
before being sold and rendered
yeoman service on the fairgrounds
until the late 1930s. This photograph, taken in 1923, shows an ex-
WD FWD lorry towing a living van
onto the tober. FWD is the maker's
name; the letters stand for four
wheel drive, and it can be seen that
full use is being made of this with
chains on all four wheels giving extra
adhesion. The lorry has been
converted into a packing truck and
carries a heavy load.

99 Transition in transport on the
fairground. Showmen arrive to set
up Mitcham Fair in the late 1920s.
Some of the loads have been brought
in by traction engine, others by
motor lorry, mainly Tilling-Stevens
and AECs. The sites, rides and stalls
have been marked out, and some of
the packing trucks are being
unloaded. On the right an Erskine
car is towing a small caravan. Trailer
car caravans made their appearance
in 1919, one of the earliest firms in
the business being Eccles who later
went on to build some for
showmen's use. The horses come
from a travelling circus which was
making up part of the show.

100 Fairgrounds were the last stronghold of the steam traction engine. Roundabout proprietors favoured them for their unfailing reliability. Further, being both big and powerful, they were capable of 'holding back' the heavy loads on gradients. John Fowler & Co (Leeds) Ltd built a special showman's diesel-engined road locomotive in 1935 for the Nottingham-based firm of Hibble & Mellors Ltd. It was appropriately named *Jubilee* because of the royal event of that year. It did not have the success anticipated, and Fowlers never built another. At that time, steam traction engines were readily available second-hand at a low price, whereas a brand-new diesel was quite an expensive item of equipment. The Fowler's ancestry is obvious from its rear wheels, which

are exactly the same as those fitted to *Supreme*, their final showman's engine built the year before. Behind the cab there is a 450/500 amp dynamo. The catalogue for this machine makes interesting reading, as it lists the many advantages of the diesel engine over the steam engine:

No driver required when generating on the fairground

No getting up steam

No picking up water on the road

No clinkering up

No plugs to drop or loss of steam at a crucial time

No washing out

No leaking tubes

No floods of water around the engine on the fairground

101 Pudding Wilson's Grand Electric Coloseum (Bioscope) in trouble at Wooler Bridge in June 1908. The engine failed to straighten up after taking a left-hand bend onto the bridge and ploughed through the parapet. Luckily, the drawbar between the engine and the first truck did not break as it was only the weight of the load which prevented the Fowler engine No 10328 *Dawn of the Century* from plunging into the river.

102 One of the most serious accidents to befall a showman's engine and road train was this one in County Durham, when the engine plunged through a wall into Park Dene valley when travelling from Burnopfield to Rowlands Gill, in 1923. The apparent carnage behind the engine has been caused by the truck containing all the animals from a set of Gallopers having burst open on impact, scattering the ride all over the valley. Unfortunately the driver of the engine was killed.

ACCIDENT AT WOOLER BRIDGE JUNE 8 1908

103 Considering the thousands of miles travelled by the fairs each year, there were very few accidents on the road. In the days of steam, when an engine with a load behind it did get out of control the results were usually spectacular. In this case a complete road train—traction engine, living van and two other trailers—has plunged off the road into the lake at Thirlmere, in June 1908, killing the driver. The Burrell Showman's Engine 2979 *Reliance* was completely submerged in the lake. This is the start of the rescue operation, with private possessions being salvaged from the living wagon. The engine involved in the accident belonged to Relph and Pedley and was only three months old. It was salvaged and sent 'in pieces' to the Thetford manufacturers who rebuilt and repaired it; it emerged as No 3038 and was renamed *The Prince* for Reuben Holdsworth's Flying Pigs and Waltzing Balloons.

104 The well known West Country Showmen Anderton & Rowland ran two fairs and a fleet of Burrell showman's engines. Here No 3833 *Queen Mary* is in trouble in the middle of Torquay, on the way to Plymouth. It skidded into a shop and blocked the road. The driver was uninjured, and there were no other casualties. The date was July 1935. The correct procedure for taking a heavy road train down a hill would be to have the brakeman apply the brakes on the loads, and then for the engine literally to pull the load down the hill against the brakes. It would appear from the form this accident has taken that the brakes were not firmly applied, and the load has tried to overtake the engine, pushing it sideways across the road, and wedging it between the shops.

103

104

105 Arnold Brothers' fair was one of the few which regularly travelled the Isle of Wight and they had their winter quarters there as well. This fair spent part of the year on the mainland, necessitating two crossings of the Solent every season. There were no drive-on, drive-off ferries in those days; just a train of barges towed by tugboat. Great driving skill was needed to load these barges, as everthing had to be pushed on backwards down the slipway and up a ramp onto the barge; as can be seen in this photograph taken in 1927, clearances were very small. Showmen's engines were also transported in this way, and it is interesting to see that the Chairoplane truck on the right-hand side was an even heavier item, weighing no less than twenty-two tons. Occasionally disaster struck. There are reputed to be six brand-new 1920 cars in the Solent, the result of a collision between the ferry and another ship on the Lymington-Yarmouth run. George Baker and Sons of Southampton lost a complete set of Gallopers in the same way on the rival Portsmouth-Ryde route in 1908.

106 During World War I the Government requisitioned traction engines, complete with drivers, and put them to work on official contracts. In many cases, they were involved in hauling gravel for building army camps and road making, and hauling stores from railway stations to the camps. Many showmen had their engines taken over as in this case, where W. Cole & Sons' three-speed Wallis & Steevens No 7052 *Morning Star* is being used to carry horses' fodder from Wool Station in Dorset to Bovington Camp. Though the engine still carries its showman's lettering on the canopy, the dynamo has been removed in the interests of lightness.

106

Living Waggons

107 The showman's waggon was his home; though some of the wealthier ones might have houses to live in during the winter, almost without exception they travelled in caravans while on the road. A simple waggon might have cost as little as £100, but the average price must have been nearer £1,000. Originally, as in this pre-World War I example, they were designed to be pulled by horses. Due to the relatively poor state of the roads, they had large wooden wheels. Both inside and outside would be highly decorated, the showmen developing their own folk art in much the same way as the gypsies or canal boatmen. Braking is only on the rear wheels and the brake shoe (which operates on the metal tyre) is plainly visible.

108 Some vans were so highly decorated that the paintwork had to be protected from the sun in the summer by canvas sheeting hung down over the sides, as in this example in the 1920s. In many cases, this sheeting was only lifted on very special occasions to show the splendours of the highly varnished paintwork and gold leaf underneath. Note the beautiful cut-glass windows. The clerestory roof, sometimes known as a 'Mollycroft', gave greater headroom throughout the centre of the van and extra windows for ventilation. As with a modern caravan, they had to be level when stationary and the means of packing them up is clearly shown.

109 The showman's caravan or living waggon was his home. Some were really opulent such as William Murphy's van built by Orton and Spooner, which was over thirty feet long and weighed ten tons. Superbly panelled, it had an electric fire and electric radiators as well. When on the road all the ornaments, vases and other loose equipment had to be stowed away carefully in lockers to prevent breakages. The showman's wife was continually building up and taking down her own home.

110 Usually the main source of heating in a van was a 'Hostess' or similar stove. On this all cooking and baking would be done, no doubt using coal which was intended for the showman's engine! Heaps of coal by the traction engine used to be sadly depleted, so Yorkshire showman Mr Waddington had his stock-pile whitewashed in an attempt to put a stop to 'coal pinching'. When one of the fair visitors asked why, Mr Waddington told him that he didn't want clouds of black smoke going into peoples' eyes!

111 Cooking was seldom done out of doors, but here at a northern fair around 1910 we see that the 'Hostess' has been taken outside and is in use at the back of one of the shows. Drinking water was a problem at any fair, the showmen having to carry it in large containers such as the galvanised one on the left. Nowadays these are often of polished stainless steel or have been chromium plated.

112 Barnet Fair in 1919 saw a large and varied collection of living waggons. Most of these are still horse-drawn, some being very simple affairs while others show the wealth of their owners. None appear to be fitted with the outside kitchen which became common when solid fuel stoves for heating and cooking gave way to paraffin and primus stoves for cooking only. It would also appear that some of the canvas-covered packing trucks were used by the gaff lads for sleeping quarters. Where a waggon had no windows on one side, if often meant that the van would be used as the backwall of a sideshow, such as a Shooter.

113 Funerals of fairground travellers are always attended by large numbers of relatives and friends, many of whom travel great distances in order to pay their last respects. Floral tributes are invariably numerous and beautiful. Reports of such funerals often occupy many columns in the showman's weekly newspaper *The World's Fair*. Often a caravan would remain empty for a long time after a funeral before the family settled into it again. In some cases it might even be sold and another one bought instead.

114 While the packing truck was primarily designed for moving the various loads of the fair on the road, it could also double up as sleeping quarters for some of the workmen. This Swinging Boat packing truck belonged to Arnold Brothers and contained living quarters for up to six hands. It carried 102 pieces belonging to the Swinging Boat, all the poles for a Coconut Sheet, a complete darts stall, a skittle stall, a round stall and a small arcade, plus ladder, steps and ball boxes, and is seen at Mill Hill, Cowes, Isle of Wight in 1932.

Permanent Fairground Sites

12.217. GENERAL VIEW OF THE PLEASURE BEACH

115 The traditional site for the permanent amusement park is at one of the popular seaside resorts, where the fair is often situated very close to the beach, as here at Great Yarmouth. Showmen who do not have travelling in their blood prefer this type of site. The takings are steady and they do not have the problems associated with moving about and continual building up and pulling down. Some seaside sites allow the rides to stay built up all through the year; others have to be cleared each autumn. Here we see, in the background, a Mountain Glide and a compact Figure of Eight version of the Big Dipper. In the foreground is a Heyday, a version of the Swirl or Whip, where series of spinning cars are propelled around a centre platform and allowed to skid outwards on the corners. The rider had no control over the cars but often the moneytakers would give cars a hefty push to build up more swing. On the right is a slot-machine arcade, something more often associated with the seaside and the pier than with travelling fairs.

116

117

116 The permanent amusement park allows the showman much more scope for his rides and machines. They can be much larger than those of the travelling fair, and do not have to be regularly dismantled. The British Empire Exhibition, Wembley, held in 1924, the like of which is unlikely to be seen again, was such a tremendous success that it remained open for another year. The Amusement Park was a real highlight and proved immensely popular, its skyline dominated by this great Racer, more often known as the Big Dipper. Patrons travelled on cars, sometimes singly or, as in this case, in trains. The cars were transported up to the top of the ride by a moving rack system, and then let go. Often they continued only by gravity, the downward speed being enough to take them over the next hump. On some of the longer rides they were again assisted up some of the steeper slopes. The space under the racer is also well employed; in the foreground was the River Caves, an underground trip by boat through artificial grottos.

117 One of the attractions often to be found on the permanent amusement site is the Miniature Railway. Here at the Great Exhibition at Wembley we see a typical example. Though in this case the Railway was sponsored during the Exhibition by the Canadian Pacific Railway, the engines and rolling stock were decidedly British. The engine is a $9\frac{1}{4}$in gauge Great Northern Atlantic originally operating on a line at Staughton Manor, owned by J.E.P. Howey who, with Count Louis Zborowski, founded the Romney, Hythe & Dymchurch Railway in Kent. The late J.A. Holder bought the engine in 1925 and operated it at Wembley as the Treasure Island Railway. The name of the engine at that time was *Peter Pan.* Later in life the engine ran on a private railway on the author's home territory at Beaulieu. The owner, Terence Holder, who is seen driving in this photograph, is still actively connected with steam preservation on the Dart Valley Railway.

118 One of the largest Big Wheels ever erected in this country was built at Earls Court, London, for the Exhibition of 1894. It was known, not unnaturally, as the Great Wheel. It had no less than forty cars and could carry two hundred people; the problems of loading and unloading the cars can be imagined. It was driven by two 50hp motors and measured 280ft in diameter. A similar wheel was erected in Vienna.

119

119 The Kursaal has long been the playground of Londoners visiting Southend-on-Sea. Here, in 1921, we see patrons enjoying the Tubs—a circular ride on which the Tubs are propelled around the centre of the machine with the top part of the Tub containing the patron, being made to spin by contact with the inside walls. As can be seen, the Tubs can also tilt. The notices or 'gag cards' are a good example of methods used to attract patrons to a ride. One would have thought that it would have been most uncomfortable to have a 'spoon by the light of the moon' on a revolving tilting Tub.

120 One of the most unusual machines at the Wembley Exhibition in 1924, was called the Whirl of the World. Here, discs revolved within the floor, spinning in different directions, so throwing the riders in their small cars away in different directions. A certain amount of braking and steering could be undertaken by the rider with the aid of the centre lever.

121 One of the most impressive machines ever to be presented on any British fairground was the Flying Machine. This was a much grander version of the Chairoplanes and could only be built up on a permanent site. The holiday makers rode in suspended cars, rather like the gondolas of an airship. This is the holiday resort of Southport in 1909. On the left is a water chute; the thrill of hurtling down the slope and hitting the water in a huge spray can be imagined. On some similar rides, spectators could view the cars hitting the water in close-up from behind a plate-glass window. Most of these spectators would scream and instinctively duck when they saw the bow-wave from the boat approaching them. The glass barrier of course kept them dry.

Index